Spiration of Love

Entering the Seven Dwellings of Heaven
Through Purgation

By Victoria Rose Pisano

Halo ●●●●
Publishing International
www.halopublishing.com

Spiration of Love

Last Discourse

Do not let your hearts be troubled.

Have faith in God and faith in me.

In my Father's house there are many dwelling places.

Entering the Seven Dwellings of Heaven Through Purgation

By Victoria Rose Pisano

This book is a further understanding to my first book
Straight Street to Heaven

For more information, contact the author:

Victoria Rose Pisano
Telephone: 440-886-5774
Email Author at: straightstreet1@cox.net
Website: www.straightstreettoheaven.com

Library of Congress Control Number: 2009929806
ISBN 978-1-935268-03-1

Halo ●●●●
Publishing International
www.halopublishing.com

Printed in the United States of America

This book is dedicated to all of my family members:

To my husband Patrick, with whom God has joined me
as friend and mate to walk this life in God

To my four children, Lisa, David, Dominic, and Patrick

I also want to dedicate this book to all of my
Straight Street Family members who took the prayer class
and shared their lives with me in Jesus

May all of you know how much I care about you and love you!

I pray that all those who read this book will have a deeper
understanding of the purging process we go through to be transformed
and to enter our baptismal life of Union, the Unblemished Lamb.

Jesus Christ Our Lord …!

Matt. 7: 7-8

Ask, and you will receive. Seek, and you will find.
Knock and it will be opened to you. For the one who asks, receives.
For the one who seeks, finds. The one who knocks, enters.

John 12: 24-26

Jesus answered them, "The hour has come for the
Son of Man to be glorified.
Amen, amen, I say to you, unless a grain of
wheat falls to the ground and dies,
it remains a grain of wheat; but if it dies,
it produces much fruit. Whoever loves his life loses it, and
whoever hates his life in this world will preserve it for eternal life.
Whoever serves me must follow me, and where I am,
there also will my servant be.
The Father will honor whoever serves me.

John 14: 1-3

He is the way, the truth and the life, says the Lord;
no one comes to the Father, except through Jesus.

Pick up your cross and follow Jesus all the way home . . .

Spiration of Love

Entering the Seven Dwellings of Heaven
Through Purgation

Lamb of God
Who Takes Away the Sins of the World

Spiration of Love

Entering the Seven Dwellings of Heaven
Through Purgation

Lamb of God
Who Takes Away the Sins of the World

Revelation 2:7

Anyone who is willing to hear should listen to the Spirit and understand what the Spirit is saying to the churches. Everyone who is victorious will eat from the tree of life in the Garden of God

Each dwelling has a secret intimate garden that we must enter to be with Jesus. In these gardens, we become transformed into His image and likeness. The deeper we enter these interior dwellings, the deeper we encounter union in Christ Jesus. By becoming one in Spirit, we enter into the marriage of the two Spirits, becoming one in mind, body, soul, and divinity. We enter the complete life of the Triune God. Each dwelling has a spiritual door except the seventh dwelling. These doors are found in the dwellings of the secret gardens deep within us. The spiritual doors are Christ Himself, and we cannot enter a new dwelling or garden until we enter as pure as Jesus, pure without any stumbling blocks or veils of darkness that keep us from entering deeper into peace and greater joy. Sin that keeps veils of darkness over our eyes blocks us from seeing God face to face. All areas of darkness in each dwelling must be removed from us for the next door to be opened by Christ Himself. The more peace and joy we have in these gardens, the less we have to be purged. If we find it is easy to enter the garden of prayer, and the garden is filled with peace, serenity, and deep joy, with little distraction, the deeper we are in Christ, and the more we are united with the Blessed Trinity. Jesus waits at the door of each dwelling. He waits for us to ask, seek, and knock. This asking and seeking and knocking is our cooperation with the Holy Spirit in the purging process. When we have cooperated fully in the dwelling we are in, and all veils of darkness and stumbling blocks have been removed in that particular dwelling, the next door is opened, leading us to the next dwelling.

This process of purification continues until we enter the seventh dwelling and can rest from all the purging.

Peter Is the Rock
Matthew 16: 13-19
When Jesus went into the region of Caesarea Philippi, he asked his disciples, "Who do you say that the Son of Man is?" They replied, "Some say John the Baptist, others Elijah, still others Jeremiah or one of the prophets." He said to them, "But who do you say that I am?" Simon Peter said in reply, "You are the Messiah, the Son of the living God." Jesus said to him in reply, "Blessed are you, Simon son of Jonah. For flesh and blood has not revealed this to you, but my heavenly Father. And so I say to you, you are Peter, and upon this rock I will build my church, and the gates of the netherworld shall not prevail against it. I will give you the keys to the kingdom of heaven. Whatever you bind on Earth shall be bound in heaven; and whatever you loose on Earth shall be loosed in heaven."

These doors will not open if we remain in pride, justifying sin and the behavior of sin. This is what Lucifer did. His arrogance and refusal to become obedient led him to fall out of Heaven. God is God, we are not God! We must listen and work with the Holy Spirit to help Him purge us so that we enter our inheritance of union in the Blessed Trinity. When we enter the secret gardens in these dwellings, the Holy Spirit will show us what needs to be purged in us. We must listen and obey and then go to the Sacraments to be healed and united to Christ. When we cooperate in this way throughout the dwelling we are in, Abba becomes very pleased with us, and the next door opens for us to proceed forth to a deeper and more intimate dwelling in Christ Jesus.

Revelation 1:17-18
When I saw him, I fell at his feet as dead. But he laid his right hand on me and said, "Don't be afraid! I am the First and the Last. I am the living one who died. Look, I am alive forever and ever! And I hold the keys of death and the grave.

A Pure Soul
Revelation 22:14-15
Blessed are those who wash their robes so they can enter through the gates of the city and eat the fruit from the tree of life. Outside the city are the dogs—the sorcerers, the sexually immoral, the murderers, the idol worshipers, and all who love to live a lie.

Revelation 1:12-14
Then I turned to see whose voice it was that spoke to me, and when I turned, I saw seven gold lamp stands and in the midst of the lamp stands one like a son of man, wearing an ankle-length robe, with a gold sash around his chest. The hair of his head was as white as white wool or as snow, and his eyes were like a fiery flame.

All seven gardens are entered through purity, so we enter Heaven in the same state as the unblemished Lamb of God, Jesus. We must take on the divine nature of the unblemished Lamb to keep entering deeper and deeper into purity. This is why the Holy Spirit purges us to transform us back into Jesus' image and likeness until the image and likeness is perfected, as when we entered Baptism: Holy as God is holy, pure as the unblemished Lamb of God, and innocent as the dove who is the love between the Father and the Son.

John 6: 54-58
He who feeds on my flesh and drinks my blood has life eternal, and I will raise him up on the last day. For my flesh is real food and my blood real drink. The man who feeds on my flesh and drinks my blood remains in me, and I in him. Just as the Father who has life sent me" and I have life because of the Father, so the man who feeds on me will have life because of me. This is the bread that came down from heaven. Unlike your ancestors who ate and died nonetheless, the man who feeds on this bread shall live forever."

Each dwelling becomes more illuminating. In each dwelling stands a golden lamp to illuminate the way, the truth, and the life of Christ within us. Each dwelling reveals the truths of what we need to do and what purging needs to be done to become purer to enter a deeper dwelling. All dwellings are also called houses or mansions. In Revelations, the symbolic word for these dwellings is "cups."

All seven cups that are symbolic of the seven dwellings are taken up during Mass and placed on the altar. Everyone who is baptized and attending Mass is being transformed through the consecration of the bread and wine and is being elevated in the life of Christ through the workings of the Holy Spirit. All of us who are in full attendance at Mass enter the seventh dwelling through this transformation, to rest in Abba as Abba is resting. This rest we enter in Abba through Eucharist is the same rest that Abba entered when He created the Heavens and the Earth in six days and rested from all that He created on the seventh day. Throughout the Liturgy of the Mass, we are being elevated into the risen Lord to be transformed in Christ through the workings of the Holy Spirit. When we enter deeper into Abba's first intention for us to enter this rest with Him, we experience all the goodness that He created.

The Blessed Trinity is revealing itself to us by the love of the Holy Spirit and His Divine Mission to purify and sanctify us and to bring us all into union in Christ. Christ and His Divine Mission are to deliver us into Abba, and it is in Abba that we enter into glory, to rest in His glory for all of eternity.

This Divine Plan of God is the opening up of Heaven through the workings of the Blessed Trinity for all who are attending the Holy Mass.

All who are attending are given Grace to be filled and to be strengthened in the Fruited Life of Christ. After the celebration of Eucharist, we are all sent down the mountain to serve the least of our brothers and sisters, using the divine life of Grace that we received in Eucharist. We go out clothed in Christ and reflect His life, which is the Spirit of love, joy, peace, patience, kindness, goodness, faithfulness, gentleness, and self-control. All of us are called by God to reflect our Divine Mission in Him. This is His call to us to enter our sainthood and to reflect our predestined unique Divine Mission. All previous saints brought to the table of plenty their Divine Mission. Their Divine Mission was revealed to us and left for us to grow and be strengthened in.

We too must live out our Divine Mission to fill the table of plenty with the life of Christ that lives in us. To begin this process, we must remove every stumbling block that obstructs the light of our Divine Mission in Christ.

The Baptism of Jesus…
Matthew 3:13-17
Then Jesus went from Galilee to the Jordan River to be baptized by John. But John did not want to baptize him. "I am the one who needs to be baptized by you," he said, "so why are you coming to me?" But Jesus said, "It must be done, because you must do everything that is right." So then John baptized him. After his baptism, as Jesus came up out of the water, the Heavens were opened and he saw the Spirit of God descending like a dove and settling on him. And a voice from Heaven said, "This is my beloved Son, and I am fully pleased with him."

God the Father is well pleased with Jesus. By cooperating with the Holy Spirit and remaining in our Baptismal state of purity, we remain in Jesus and become pleasing to God the Father. The heavens remain open, for God sees in us the perfect image and likeness of His only begotten Son whom we inherited in our Baptism.

Pick Up Your Cross and Follow Christ
Matthew 16: 24-27

Then Jesus said to the disciples, "If any of you wants to be my follower, you must put aside your selfish ambition, Pick up your cross, and follow me. If you try to keep your life for yourself, you will lose it. But if you give up your life for me, you will find true life. And how do you benefit if you gain the whole world but lose your own soul in the process? Is anything worth more than your soul? For I, the Son of Man, will come in the glory of my Father with his angels and will judge all people according to their deed.

As we enter the first dwelling to come back to our Heavenly Father, we must repent and reform our lives back into the image and likeness of Jesus Christ, the state we inherited in Baptism. This reformation must be entered with a complete conversion of heart and life. We must love God with our whole heart, mind, soul, and strength, and love our neighbors as ourselves. As we proceed up the mountain of transfiguration to be purified by the Holy Spirit, let us follow the life of our Lord Jesus Christ so that all may know, love, and serve Him as Savior of the world.

All of our missions are to proceed up this mountain to be transformed into Christ and enter God's glory. Once we enter a higher or deeper dwelling, Christ needs us to make the turn and proceed down the mountain to reflect His glory. His reflection that illuminates through us is God's glory, and it is by this glory that others are called to Him. This turn is our way of serving our brothers and sisters in Christ and to encourage and to strengthen them so that they too can begin their journey up the transforming mountain.

Jesus told His apostles, "You are not here to be served, you are here to serve." We must serve our brothers and sisters in Christ through His glory so that they can begin to see through the darkness and enter deeper into His glorifying light.

Pick Up Your Cross and Follow Jesus

Lamb of God
Who Takes Away the Sins of the World

The First Dwelling of Purgatory

The First Door Opens: Jesus Says, "Come Forward!"

Jesus came into the world to bring us back into paradise so that we can once again rest in God as God is resting in us through our Baptism. He takes us through these mansions until we enter the highest mansion.

The Many Dwellings in Heaven
John 14: 1-3, 11-21

In my Father's house there are many dwelling places. Do not let your hearts be troubled. You have faith in God; have faith also in me. In my Father's house there are many dwelling places. If there were not, would I have told you that I am going to prepare a place for you? And if I go and prepare a place for you, I will come back again and take you to myself, so that where I am you also may be. Where (I) am going you know the way. Believe me that I am in the Father and the Father is in me, or else, believe because of the works themselves. Amen, amen, I say to you, whoever believes in me will do the works that I do, and will do greater ones than these, because I am going to the Father. And whatever you ask in my name, I will do, so that the Father may be glorified in the Son. If you ask anything of me in my name, I will do it. If you love me, you will keep my commandments. And I will ask the Father, and he will give you another Advocate to be with you always, the Spirit of truth, which the world cannot accept, because it neither sees nor knows it. But you know it because it remains with you, and will be in you. I will not leave you orphans; I will come to you. In a little while the world will no longer see me, but you will see me, because I live and you will live. On that day you will realize that I am in my Father and you are in me and I in you. Whoever has my commandments and observes them is the one who loves me. And whoever loves me will be loved by my Father, and I will love him and reveal myself to him.

Because we live in a world that does not fully understand the promise of our Baptismal lives in the Blessed Trinity, we grow up in a world that lives in darkness. We are tricked into thinking that the way of the flesh is the good way, so we try to fulfill every desire that is not God's desire. The result is living in darkness instead of living in His light as children of the light. God's desire is to have us home with Him in Heaven. As we grow in a world that is filled with darkness, we once again lose our way in God and begin to pick off the wrong tree, the tree of bad knowledge. We try to fill our lives with false gods that only please the flesh instead of the spirit of truth.

This wrong way that we have learned to walk is the story of Adam and Eve repeated. The result is that we lose our way in our Baptismal life.

This story is like the prodigal story in the Bible. The young son takes his inheritance and spends it on loose living and enters deeper and deeper into despair and sin. We, like the young son, must return to our Father's house in all of His goodness. If we remain in darkness with all the false gods we worship, we are banished from entering into Heaven. Grace, God's life in us, cannot fill us if we have severed our relationship with God. If the relationship has been severed, we will remain in darkness. This darkness leads us away from Heaven. Christ's light of His life that we inherited in Baptism is our true image and likeness; and it is through Christ that we once again can enter Heaven, our true home, to enter rest in the glory of God forever.

How Man and Woman Left Heaven
Gen. 3: 21-24
For the man and his wife, the Lord God made leather garments, with which he clothed them, see! The man has become like one of us, knowing what is good and what is bad! Therefore, he must not be allowed to put out his hand to take fruit from the tree of life also and thus eat of it and live forever. The Lord God therefore banished him from the Garden of Eden, to till the ground from which he had been taken. When he expelled the man, he settled him east of the Garden of Eden; and he stationed the cherubim and the fiery revolving sword, to guard the way to the tree of life.

St. John the Baptist said, "I must decrease, Christ must increase."

How Man and Woman Enter Back into Heaven
Matthew 3: 1-3, 11- 17
In those days John the Baptist appeared, preaching in the desert of Judea (and) say-ing, "Repent, for the kingdom of heaven is at hand!" It was of him that the prophet Isaiah had spoken when he said: "A voice of one crying out in the desert, 'Prepare the

way of the Lord, make straight his paths.'" I am baptizing you with water, for repentance, but the one who is coming after me is mightier than I. I am not worthy to carry his sandals. He will baptize you with the Holy Spirit and fire. His winnowing fan is in his hand. He will clear his threshing floor and gather his wheat into his barn, but the chaff he will burn with unquenchable fire." Then Jesus came from Galilee to John at the Jordan to be baptized by him. John tried to prevent him, saying, "I need to be baptized by you, and yet you are coming to me?" Jesus said to him in reply, "Allow it now, for thus it is fitting for us to fulfill all righteousness." Then he allowed him. After Jesus was baptized, he came up from the water and behold, the heavens were opened (for him), and he saw the Spirit of God descending like a dove (and) coming upon him. And a voice came from the heavens, saying, "This is my beloved Son, with whom I am well pleased."

In this first dwelling, Jesus, as teacher and healer, heals the sickness of death that lives in us and schools us into knowing Him as He is—holy, pure, and innocent. Our weak selves need to be strengthened and sustained in the Life of Christ, so we begin by filling ourselves with Grace. We who need to be strengthened and sustained in the life of Grace need to remain faithful to the Catholic Church and all her teachings. This life of Sacrament fills us with the life of Christ, which is called Sacramental Grace.

Sacramental Grace keeps us purified and transformed in the life of Christ, and it is through this transformation in Christ that we are able to remain in our Baptismal life.

Hail Mary full of Grace, the Lord is with you, blessed are you amongst women, and blessed is the Fruit of your womb, Jesus…

In pondering these words in the Hail Mary, we now know that we, too, must be filled with Grace.

Learning to Know God…!
GEN 2: 16-17
The Lord God gave man this order: "You are free to eat from any of the trees of the garden except the tree of knowledge of good and bad. From that tree you shall not eat; the moment you eat from it you are surely doomed to die."

We as humans dwell in different states as we grow in God. The curtain was torn from top to bottom when Christ died. The different states we live in-as we journey through these purgation dwellings can be lived in from the top of Heaven, our elevated lives in Christ, to the bottom of hell, where God is not present. Those who dwell in hell learn and desire all the evil knowledge of this world. Their state makes everything a god, except the true and only God. So the soul who is walking on Earth now but dwells in hell must make a complete conversion back to the promises of Baptism. This conversion begins with filling the soul with the good knowledge of God and all that He desires for us to become the saints that He intended us to be. In the first dwelling of purgation, God desires us more than we desire Him. It is in this first dwelling that He brings the soul back to the good knowledge of His creation. This good knowledge brings the soul to the understanding of the life in Christ that we inherited when the fullness of the Blessed Trinity entered into our souls on the day of our Baptism. On this day, the Blessed Trinity became one with us, making us a temple of the living God. The soul grows in this good knowledge of God that we enter through the Baptismal waters. The soul begins a journey in Christ and walks up the mountain into a deeper more intimate relationship with Jesus.

It is in the next three dwellings that God schools the soul on how to know Him. This knowing brings the soul deeper into loving God. When the soul learns how to love God, He brings the soul into knowing how to love Him by serving Him in others. The walk up the mountain begins with schooling the soul in good knowledge. This schooling in good knowledge allows the soul to enter a deeper understanding of the way God works in His body, the Church. What we now learn, we must put into practice, for our words and our deeds must be in complete harmony to become the perfect saint in Christ. Let us go up the mountain through, with, and in Jesus, to be transformed in Love…!

The Fulfillment of All Commandments . . .
 As we begin this journey up the mountain to live full lives in Jesus, we must keep in mind two important lessons that Jesus taught us. First, we must love God with our whole heart, mind, soul, and strength. Second, we must love our neighbors as ourselves. Jesus expects us to serve the least of our brothers and sisters. For whatever we do for the least of them, we are doing for Him

In The Upper Room, Jesus Teaches Us the "Turn Around."
Luke 22: 31
Simon, Simon, behold Satan has demanded to sift all of you like wheat, but I have prayed that your own faith may not fail; and once you have turned back, you must strengthen your brothers.

At the end of the first dwelling, we must make this turn. This turn requires us to go down the mountain where we once dwelt and minister to those who are younger or still living in hell with all their false gods. If we remember, when we first entered our conversion back to God, someone ministered to us to bring us into our conversion. So we must help our sisters and brothers who are lost to find their way back home in Christ. This turn-around is required of us through all seven dwellings to serve the needs of those who are dwelling in the shallower dwellings. This turn and all it requires in us is our perfect walk in Christ and must be carried out to the fullest through all seven dwellings.

As We Receive, We Give Back . . .

The more we are filled with the life of God, the more we are expected to make this turn down the mountain to help fill the needs of those who are least in the kingdom of God. We must fill their needs as our needs were filled, with the good knowledge of our Baptismal life in Christ Jesus. This good knowledge will let them know they are already saved in the life of God. Helping them will lead them to understand what they must do to cooperate with the workings of the Holy Spirit and to rise up to the life of dignity that we all share in the life of Jesus. When we minister to those who are in the first dwelling of purgation, we must come down the mountain with all the Fruits of the Holy Spirit: love, joy, peace, patience, kindness, goodness, gentleness, and self-control. The "old" we who walked out of self-ego must decrease, and the life of Christ in us must increase. This decreasing in self continues as we walk up the mountain until we, along with St. Paul, can say, "It is no longer I that live but Christ through me." Be Perfect As Christ Is Perfect...

This perfect way to walk in our Christian lives is to walk in the perfection and goodness of Christ Jesus, with whom the Father is well pleased. The deeper we enter Christ, the more we will reflect Christ through us in all His perfection. Our part in the Life of the Blessed Trinity is to cooperate as our Blessed Mother did and to say *yes* to God. We must cooperate with the Divine Mission through the workings of the Holy Spirit, to help Him purge us of all the false gods that we brought into our lives. These false gods have blocked the light of Christ in our lives.

For Those He Foreknew He Also Predestined...
Rom 8:28-30
Brothers and sisters: We know that all things work for good for those who love God, who are called according to his purpose. For those he foreknew he also predestined to be conformed to the image of his Son so that he might be the firstborn among many brothers and sisters. And those he predestined he also called; and those he called he also justified; and those he justified he also glorified.

When we entered our Baptismal life in Christ Jesus, we entered our predestined life in Him, which is our sanctified life or our sainthood. It is His will in our predestined life in Christ Jesus that we are to bring light to the Earth as it is in Heaven.

Luke 23: 34
Jesus said, "Father forgive them: they do not know what they are doing."

This first dwelling is where one begins to see how weak in the Holy Spirit we are without the Grace to help sustain us. This weakness is from a lack of Sacramental Grace. Because we entered the first dwelling of Purgatory, we lack Grace. We lose the life of Grace that once filled us in Baptism. Our interior soul becomes depleted and is in a weak, sick, blind state. This same state is seen in Saul, when he realized whom he was persecuting. This blindness and sickness caused by sin can be healed if we begin to go to the Sacraments consistently. This Grace of God's life strengthens us to become what God called us to become, sanctified! God predestined us to be sanctified in Christ Jesus as saints. This sainthood is the life we receive in the Sacrament of Baptism. This is also the life Jesus delivers to us when we enter the Sacrament of the Eucharist. Each Sacrament we enter strengthens us in the life we are trying to enter.

There will be many obstacles in this first dwelling. All evil will try to influence us to give up this life in Jesus. All the evil we encounter in this first dwelling is our old life of sin. The obstacles or stumbling blocks we created that kept us away from God are now the obstacles and stumbling blocks we must remove to have a path to Jesus. What we are fighting against is evil. Every time we demonstrate self-control by not reflecting sinful behavior, we give birth to Christ who lives in us through our Baptism. All the Fruits of God's life living in us need to be given birth, so that we as Christians will reflect the spirit of love, joy, peace, patience, kindness, goodness, faithfulness, gentleness and self-control. Put away the old behavior and give birth to Jesus for the world to see so that others may come into the illumination of His life and give Him the glory He deserves.

John 3: 16
For God so loved the world that He gave His only begotten Son, that whoever believes in Him shall not perish, but have eternal life.

Areas in us that need to increase in the first dwelling:

- A knowing of being adopted and loved by all of Heaven
- A return to true happiness deep within our souls
- A sense of freedom from what kept us bonded to evil prior to our return to God's mercy and love
- A re-awakening of our birth in Baptism

- Great conversion (a return to feeling good about ourselves) Great humility because of the awareness of the way we once lived without Christ in our lives
- A true desire to repent and reform our lives
- Tremendous sorrow for sin
- Removal of all objects and thoughts that led us to sin
- Buying holy Sacramental objects that represent our new lives in Jesus
- Fasting from food to discipline the flesh
- New spiritual friends
- Great trials and tribulations because evil is trying to hold onto us
- A cleansing of our old lives to reflect our new lives in Christ Jesus
- Patience with others who are not cooperating in the life of Grace
- Growth in all the Fruits of God's life in us: love, joy, peace, patience, kindness, goodness, faithfulness, gentleness, and self-control
- A desire to have joy and peace
- Feelings of being holy and renewed
- A desire to volunteer at local parishes
- A need to purify the outside of the cup, meaning that we need to change our actions and begin to reflect the actions of someone who is living his faith in Christ Jesus
- A need to discipline the flesh to dwell deeper in the life of the Holy Spirit

Areas in us that need to be purged in the first dwelling

- Shallow desires that feed and fill the ego instead of filling the will of God in your life
- Living in emotions that peek our feelings (These high peaks and low valleys of emotions have to be evened out to reflect the peace of Christ.)
- Shallow thinking that no matter what we do in life, we are doing God's will (This is pride and this sort of thinking has to decrease.)
- Walking through life on feelings with little faith (We think that this is how everyone walks in Christ.)
- Jumping from the desire to be in Jesus back to earthly desires
- Inconsistency in faith

Since Satan has tricked us into worshiping false gods by deceiving us in power, lust, and greed, we must turn away from his empty temptations and once again follow Christ to find our one and only true God. In this first dwelling, we must learn good knowledge that will bring us to know God as God is—all good. Good knowledge will keep us rooted and firm in our Catholic Faith. So it is in this dwelling that we need to learn all about our Faith.

Buying a catechism of the Catholic Faith and reading books about the lives of the saints will inspire us and strengthen us to follow Jesus up the mountain.

The first three dwellings teach us to know God with all our hearts.

Spiritual Notes

*Lamb of God
Who Takes Away the Sins of the World*

The Second Dwelling of Purgatory:

The Second Door Opens: Jesus Says, "Come Forward!"

Mark 7:14-23
He summoned the crowd again and said to them, "Hear me, all of you, and understand.
Nothing that enters one from outside can defile that person; but the things that come out from within are what defile." When he got home away from the crowd his disciples questioned him about the parable. He said to them, "Are even you likewise without understanding? Do you not realize that everything that goes into a person from outside cannot defile, since it enters not the heart but the stomach and passes out into the latrine?" (Thus he declared all foods clean.) "But what comes out of a person, that is what defiles. From within people, from their hearts, come evil thoughts, un chastity, theft, murder, adultery, greed, malice, deceit, licentiousness, envy, blasphemy, arrogance, folly. All these evils come from within and they defile."

Repent and reform from your old ways.

St. Paul's Conversion and Ours
ACTS 9:1-20
Saul, still breathing murderous threats against the disciples of the Lord, went to the high priest and asked him for letters to the synagogues in Damascus, that, if he should find any men or women who belonged to the Way, he might bring them back to Jerusalem in chains. On his journey, as he was nearing Damascus, a light from the sky suddenly flashed around him. He fell to the ground and heard a voice saying to him, "Saul, Saul, why are you persecuting me?" He said, "Who are you, sir?" The reply came, "I am Jesus, whom you are persecuting. Now get up and go into the city and you

will be told what you must do." The men who were traveling with him stood speechless, for they heard the voice but could see no one. Saul got up from the ground, but when he opened his eyes he could see nothing; so they led him by the hand and brought him to Damascus. For three days he was unable to see, and he neither ate nor drank. There was a disciple in Damascus named Ananias, and the Lord said to him in a vision, "Ananias." He answered, "Here I am, Lord." The Lord said to him, "Get up and go to the street called Straight and ask at the house of Judas for a man from Tarsus named Saul. He is there praying, and in a vision he has seen a man named Ananias come in and lay his hands on him, that he may regain his sight." But Ananias replied, "Lord, I have heard from many sources about this man, what evil things he has done to our holy ones in Jerusalem. And here he has authority from the chief priests to imprison all who call upon our name." But the Lord said to him, "Go, for this man is a chosen instrument of mine to carry my name before Gentiles, kings, and children of Israel, and I will show him what he will have to suffer for my name." So Ananias went and entered the house; laying his hands on him, he said,

"Saul, my brother, the Lord has sent me, Jesus who appeared to you on the way by which you came that you may regain your sight and be filled with the Holy Spirit." Immediately things like scales fell from his eyes and he regained his sight. He got up and was baptized, and when he had eaten, he recovered his strength. He stayed some days with the disciples in Damascus, and he began at once to proclaim Jesus in the synagogues, that he is the Son of God.

Blessed Are the Clean of Heart, for They Will See God.
We must decrease, so the life of Christ in us can increase ….
When entering the second dwelling, we begin to see all in us that is not of God. We can then begin to discipline ourselves in the life we live in Him. Many of us have not been to confession for a very long time because we might be fearful. Do not let this fear of revealing our sinful nature in the Sacrament of Reconciliation keep us from re-entering the Church in full Grace. As we grow in the life of Jesus, we want all the stumbling blocks that obstruct our way to Jesus to be purified. As we grew up in our natural lives, we learned the way of darkness that has kept us in confusion. It is in that confused state that the world remains in darkness. Our lives in Christ must be completely healed. We must make the complete conversion back to Him without stumbling blocks. By going to reconciliation, our soul transforms back into the image and likeness that we entered in Baptism. This perfect image and likeness is Christ Himself. Jesus asks us to pick up our cross and to follow Him.

The Cross of Christ . . .

The cross of Christ is the cross of all of our sins that crucified Him. If we follow Him, we too will pick up our cross as He did and rid ourselves of the sin that keeps us bound to Satan. We pick up our cross when we enter the confession booth and begin to repent all that crucified Christ. Sins crucified Christ as they also crucify us. By going to confession, we cleanse our souls, and the Sacrament of Reconciliation transforms us into the pure image and likeness of Jesus. In this second dwelling of purgation, we cooperate in a fuller way with the Life of the Holy Spirit living in us. His Divine Mission is to sanctify us and purify us through purgation. Unless we enter Christ as Christ is, we cannot enter our rest in Abba.

Veils of Darkness . . .

Because we have dwelled so long in darkness, our eyes have become blind to the light of Christ's life in us. There are six veils that cover our eyes, and as we enter deeper and deeper into the life of Jesus in us, Jesus begins to unveil our eyes to see Him as He is. This unveiling is bringing us deeper into the beatific vision, the beatitude: "Blessed are the pure of heart, they shall see God." These veils are evil ways that have blinded us over the years. They are the vile ways we once walked when we did not know that, by our Baptism, we enter our sanctified life, which is our sainthood in Jesus. So the deeper we enter these dwellings, the more profound our lives become in Christ.

Our Divine Mission …

When we entered the Baptismal waters, we entered the Life of Christ. So as we enter deeper and deeper into these dwellings, we begin to see that Abba has a predestined Divine Plan for us. This Divine Plan is our inherited sanctified life in Christ. He is the Tree of Life, and we are the branches. Every good tree produces much fruit. The Fruit of His Life in us is our sanctified life in Him. All saints have a sanctified Divine Mission that they inherited through Christ. This sanctified life in Christ is what they have left us on the table of plenty. We can see their sanctified lives and all that they have left us as we ponder their unique lives in Christ through the many books written about them. We also have a Divine Mission in Christ that needs to bring His light to Earth as it is in Heaven. The Fruit of God's Life in us is our sanctified life. This sanctified life in Christ Jesus brings Heavenly food to Earth. This Divine Mission reveals our life in Christ and His Life in us. All saints reveal the Full Life of the Blessed Trinity. The saints of our Church have left us the fruits of their lives in Jesus and His Life in them. Each one is unique in the Life of Jesus. As we climb the mountain of our Baptismal lives in Jesus and enter deeper into His life, this Divine Mission begins to reveal itself to us.

Abba's Will …
Any darkness that lives in us will be purified by the Holy Spirit. This purifying is the fire of Baptism. As Jesus walked this Earth in His fully human, fully God, self, He always said, "I am here to fulfill my Heavenly Father's Will." Our lives, as we climb the mountain of our Baptism, should reflect and follow that of Christ. We are here to fulfill, like Jesus, our Heavenly Father's will to become the saints God already acknowledges in us. To do God's will is to bring forth from within us this Divine Mission of His Life that we inherited in Baptism, the Divine Mission of Christ's unique Life waiting in us to be born through us. Abba already knows our Divine Mission in Christ, and it is by our cooperation through the purging process that this Divine Mission will be perfected.

Enter through the Narrow Gate
Matthew 6:
Enter through the narrow gate; for the gate is wide and the road broad that leads to destruction, and those who enter through it are many. How narrow the gate and constricted the road that leads to life. And those who find it are few.

At the crucifixion, there were two thieves on either side of Jesus. On the left was the one who justified his sinful life; he went to hell for all eternity. On the right of Jesus was the thief who repented and reformed his life; he went with Jesus into Heaven. Do not be the one who justifies sin. Be the one who repents and reforms his whole life to enter Heaven forever with Jesus.

To Make an Examination of Conscience . . .
As we think about how we offend God, we should ask God to help us to become pure and clean of Heart like His Son Jesus. We can pray that He shows us what needs to be removed from our souls that is blocking the light of our lives in Jesus. These sins we justify are stumbling blocks that are preventing us from entering into God's light. When we cannot enter God's light, we cannot be illuminated by the life of the Holy Spirit who wants to teach us the way to Jesus. By going to confession, we are lifted from the darkness of evil that keeps us in a confused state.

Evil, or Satan, would love for us to remain in this darkened state to keep us confused. Jesus in the Sacrament of Reconciliation lifts this darkness from us, and we re-enter our Baptismal state of Christ's illumination. Before entering the confessional, look over the list of Commandments and the list of mortal sins; see if you go against any Commandment of God or if you live in these mortal sins. If you do, you need to confess your sins with a complete contrite heart and vow never to repeat these sins again. Our complete, contrite heart transforms us from the sin of darkness and the effect of the sin that has kept us in confusion. This cooperation in the life of the Sacrament of Reconciliation is your call to repent and reform. You repent from darkness and reform into a child who belongs to Christ. Enter the confessional booth in a humble state. Begin with the sign of the cross.

My last confession was…?

Confess your sins; do not hide any sin or try to cover up any sin that needs to be confessed. Keep Christ Jesus and His purity & holiness as your focus. The Priest will give you a penance and perhaps some advice to keep you focused on staying pure and holy in Christ.

Act of Contrition
O my God, I am heartily sorry for having offended you and I detest all my sins because I dread the loss of Heaven and the pains of hell; but most of all because they offend you, my God, who are all good and deserving of all my love. I firmly resolve, with the help of your Grace, to confess my sins, to do penance, and to amend my life. Amen

If you do not know this act of contrition or would like to express your deep sorrow for sinning against God and ask for His Mercy, then feel free to express in your own words that which reflects your complete, contrite heart.

This is what I say when I go to confession:
"Jesus, thank you for providing me a place in this Sacrament where I can come to you and tell you how sorry I am for sinning against you. I ask you, Lord, please fill me with your Grace, and allow your light of Grace to be reflected through me. I love you, and thank you, and always praise you … Amen."

During absolution, the priest acts in the person of Christ Jesus and says the prayer of absolution. As the priest says, "I absolve you in the Name of the Father, Son, and Holy Spirit," you make the sign of the cross and know this is the same Father, Son, and Holy Spirit you entered the day of your Baptism. You are now transformed back into the image and likeness of Christ. The Priest will then dismiss you. If you have offended some person involving your sin, you must try to make amends to that person. Remember, always give your Lord thanks.

Areas in us that need to increase in the second dwelling:

- True humbleness
- Peace and joy
- A desire to volunteer in your parish
- A desire to go to daily Mass
- A desire to pray, but only certain written prayers (You are not comfortable praying with your own words from the heart yet.)
- A desire to be holy
- Deeper feelings of intimacy with our Blessed Mother
- Further withdrawal from our old lives because our former selves reflect out-of-control evil
- Turmoil in family because of our desire to change for God (This turmoil is a way God uses to bring others to move in the right direction towards Him and begin the conversion back to Him.)
- Many temptations of the flesh (Temptation sometimes makes one stronger. Temptations are like working out our weak muscles to make them stronger. This strength in Christ is needed as we travel up the mountain of transfiguration.)
- Strength to be consistent in faith
- A deeper commitment to Jesus and the life He is calling you to enter, which is your sainthood
- The ability to put our Catholic faith into action
- A desire to know that our Catholic faith deepens
- Heightened senses (In the first three dwellings, God uses our senses to enlighten our being and to become aware of His being in our midst.)
- The gathering of holy Sacramental objects. (We might begin to gather relics of saints. In the second dwelling, this is a good area, but we must watch this area in the third dwelling so it does not become a show for others to think that by wearing or owning a Sacramental that the Sacramental makes us more holy. A Sacramental is used as a reminder of holiness for us to grow in the life of Christ and to bring us deeper into the life of Grace.)

Areas in us that need to be purged in the second dwelling:

- A possible infatuation with certain priests because of what they represent—God! (This infatuation may occur because we still relate to physical holiness instead of dwelling in the Holy Spirit.)

- Fears or anxieties of not knowing what God expects of us

- A desire to dress to attract attention (The flesh in the second dwelling still needs much purging to reflect the wholeness God wants us to reflect.)

- Moving towards Jesus with feelings instead of reason or faith

- Thinking we are doing God's will by desiring to do our own will (Through the healing sacraments, God helps us to see what areas need to be purified in us. Once these areas are healed and disciplined, we naturally move forward in the life of Grace.)

- Inhibitions that keep us from being all that we need to be for Jesus (Inhibitions keep us locked in ourselves. We need to be free to serve Christ. We must look deep within ourselves to see what areas are not of God, but are of our own desires. These self-seeking desires might keep us stuck in certain areas of our lives.)

- Jumping from the flesh's desire of living loose to the Holy Spirit's desire of living as holy as God lives. (Our thinking might be that God accepts any behavior no matter what we do. We need to detach from behaviors that keep us attached to the desires of the flesh that lead us away from God.)

- Inconsistency (One minute we might be praying; the next minute we might be cussing. We lack consistency because we lack Grace and obedience and discipline.)

- Illusions that keep us bound to false joys and hopes.

- Visions that interfere with God's will (At the end of this second dwelling, we might have visions or begin to think we are seeing angels or saints. These visions stem from our desire to be as holy as God is holy. We might become stuck in thinking that we are more special than others who cannot see visions.)

The first three dwellings are of John the Baptist telling us to repent and to reform our lives. In these first three dwellings of purgation, we must decrease in habitual sin and the effects it has on us. We have become too comfortable in our old selves, and it shows up in our attitudes and the way we treat one another.

John the Baptist points the way to Christ with great instructions: *I must decrease, Christ must increase.* By uniting our wills to Abba's will, we allow Christ to increase as we decrease. In Jesus there are no stumbling blocks of sin. Sin and the effects of sin show up in our attitudes. Our loving ways still reflect much dysfunction. These dysfunctional ways of loving others must be purified by the Holy Spirit to bring us into pure, innocent Love. This Love reflects God and brings us into our true image and likeness in Christ Jesus. Be Holy as God is Holy. Be Pure as Jesus is. Be innocent as the dove who is the pure spirit of love between the Father and the Son.

Spiritual Notes

Lamb of God
Who Takes Away the Sins of the World

The Third Dwelling of Purgatory

The Third Door Opens: Jesus says, "Come Forward!"

 In the third dwelling, we begin to desire deeper prayer. This deeper prayer usually consists of rosaries, novenas, stations of the cross, attending daily Mass and going to adoration. These souls are very dedicated to our Blessed Mother who is guiding them at this point. The souls in this third dwelling are becoming very habitual in prayer. In the first and second dwelling, we worked very hard to clean up our temple, or our soul, for God. He loves the fact that we returned to Him and began the process of cleaning up our lives for Him. He loves us so much that He begins to pull us into this third dwelling; it is in this third dwelling that our senses are at their peak. God allows our senses to experience visions. Our senses are so heightened at this point that we might begin to smell beautiful roses, a scent of Heaven, a smell we never experienced before. We might even see Jesus in the Holy Eucharist. We might get visions of angels or saints, maybe even our Blessed Mother appearing to us to encourage us to keep entering deeper into these dwellings of holiness. In this third dwelling, we use our senses to try to see God and the path to Him. This dwelling is very sweet with all the good substance Heaven is made of except one thing, "faith." Most of the walk in this third dwelling is rooted in feeling good; this is what God is using to bring us forth in this third dwelling. God uses this time to strengthen us on our journey back to Him.

This third dwelling is a unique dwelling that is obvious to see. Many clothe themselves differently to show the world they are different and living a life that is pleasing to God. The pattern most people enter when they enter this third dwelling might become a little extreme. Many wear not one cross, but many. They wear many saint medals around their necks to show the world they are dedicated to God rather than to the world. Their houses might look like shrines. Statues of our Blessed Mother and statues of the saints will be everywhere. Some of these third purgatory dwellers are always fighting to change the Church, and they have a tendency to point their fingers at all the priests, binging out what the priests should be doing rather than appreciating what they are doing. The third dwellers get fixated in making sure everything is being done perfectly on the outside. They find fault with many.

We cannot skip a dwelling of purgatory. Each dwelling has its own purpose. In these first three dwellings of purgatory, we must begin to be disciplined and schooled in crucial areas that will help us become healthy and strong in Grace. In the first three dwellings of purgatory, we are experiencing the washing of water that occurs in Baptism. This washing is of John the Baptizer. The water is a symbol of the Holy Spirit washing us of all mortal sin that keeps us sick and bound to the old life of original sin. This original sin was washed away in Baptism, but because our parents or caretakers did not understand the new life we entered in Christ when we were washed clean of original sin, they believed it was natural to raise their children the way they were raised.

Many of the ways we were raised were very dysfunctional; that dysfunction passes itself down from one generation to the next. We live in the sin of learned behavior passed down to us from previous generations. Original sin that we encounter as we grow in a world that does not know Christ is passed down and reflected to innocent children. These children, once exposed to the dysfunction, learn that dysfunctional behavior. As we grow in our Earthly lives, we become slaves to the sin that makes us sick in the lives we entered in Christ Jesus. This effect of original sin keeps us in darkness, which keeps us sick in Satan and entraps us in the clutches of his darkness.

This Darkness Keeps Us Ignorant of God's Ways.
 His Gifts of wisdom, understanding, knowledge, council, fortitude, piety, and fear of the Lord are buried in us. This darkness that keeps us ignorant will eventually bring us to death. The sting of death is sin. If this learned dysfunctional behavior does not change, the soul's destination is hell forever. If we keep living in and reflecting the actions of original sin, we are allowing Satan to bring us deeper into hell. This is why our world is overshadowed in darkness. Jesus brought us into the light, and the light is dwelling in us. God's light of truth, who is the Holy Spirit, needs us to reflect His glory to bring to Earth the glory of God Himself. This glory reflects the life where God intended us to rest when creation first began. These first three dwellings are detaching us from the flesh's desires of power, lust, and greed and reforming us back to the new life we entered in Baptism. Everyone who enters the third dwelling will not always be as extreme as I have explained. Those who have the most childhood wounds are the ones who are most likely to become stuck in this dwelling and refuse to move on. The deeper the childhood

wounds, the deeper they dwell in the dysfunctional behavior that holds them bound to this dwelling. Many people in this third dwelling begin to have dreams. Dreams are God's way of guiding us closer to Him. They also warn us of some areas in our lives that might hurt us; they confirm in us our way to God. These confirmation dreams help increase our faith in Christ Jesus.

Dreams That Direct and Guide Us . . .
We might have dreams telling us what we must do to grow closer to God. We might have dreams of our loved ones or saints who are guiding us closer to Jesus.

Dreams That Warn Us . . .
We might have dreams to show us what we need to detach from our lives. These areas of darkness in us are the areas that block us from entering Christ more deeply. They are like vices that so many justify as a false god that covers up the truth that one refuses to see. For example, a person may take unlimited prescription drugs or alcohol to numb pain that might have stemmed from childhood wounds that were afflicted upon them. The pain of these wounds may be attached to a bad memory of some sort of abuse. Instead of dealing with the bad memory and the abuse and allowing God to heal him of the bad memory, the person continues to take medication to cover up the pain. Dreams reveal to us the ways we are killing ourselves. God, in all of His goodness, directs us through the workings of the Holy Spirit to the pain, so that we can deal with the truth even if it hurts and give up the vice before the vice leads us to greater sickness and pain. This pain could lead us to death instead of life. Dreams are God's way to reveal in us what we may have repressed when we were still small children. He needs these repressed memories that hinder us on our way to Him to be healed. Dreams also are a way we bring to the surface the truth that is within us.

Dreams to Confirm Our Way to Him . . .
Many times we dream of those who have passed and are smiling at us or hugging us. I call these dreams "confirming dreams." God allows us to have them to encourage and strengthen us on our way to Him.

The Promise of the Spirit...
Joel 2:28
It will come about after this. That I will pour out My Spirit on all mankind; and our sons and daughters will prophesy, our old men will dream dreams, and our young men will see visions.

The Third Heaven
2 Corinthians 12: 1-9
I must boast; not that it is profitable, but I will go on to visions and revelations of the Lord. I know someone in Christ who, fourteen years ago (whether in the body or out of the body I do not know, God knows), was caught up to the third Heaven. And I know that this person (whether in the body or out of the body I do not know, God knows) was caught up into Paradise and heard ineffable things, which no one may utter. About this person I will boast, but about myself I will not boast, except about my weaknesses. Although if I should wish to boast, I would not be foolish, for I would be telling the truth. But I refrain, so that no one may think more of me than what he sees in me or hears from me because of the abundance of the revelations. Therefore, that I might not become too elated, a thorn in the flesh was given to me, an angel of Satan, to beat me, to keep me from being too elated. Three times I begged the Lord about this, that it might leave me, but he said to me, "My Grace is sufficient for us, for power is made perfect in weakness." I will rather boast most gladly of my weaknesses, in order that the power of Christ may dwell with me.

The Voice of Symbolism . . .
In this third dwelling, God allows our natural senses to be fully opened. We begin to experience God in everything. In this dwelling, God has our natural senses peaking, so that we can feel Him near to us. He allows these strong senses to strengthen us, so that when we enter deeper into faith, in the fourth dwelling, we will have recall of what we experienced in the third dwelling. This third dwelling and all the wonderful moments one has here as God is revealing Himself to the soul strengthen us for the fourth dwelling. The reading about St. Paul entering into the third dwelling describes the wonders of Heaven that we might enter in our intimate lives in Jesus through prayer. God makes Himself known through everything that is created by Him. In this dwelling, we begin to symbolically hear His voice, like the woman at the well who was talking about the well water, while Jesus was talking about the water that would well up inside of her if she were baptized. In the third dwelling, we begin to hear Jesus speak to us in symbolic speech through the Holy Spirit. This way of knowing deepens our understanding and our knowledge in God. This secret language is now being revealed to us as St. Paul describes in this reading. We are diving deeper into the life of Jesus, and He begins to reveal in us His Truths.

Every Breath We Breathe . . .
Every breath we breathe is God. So everything that was created by Him is good.

Why God Allows Us to Have Visions . . .

Visions are God's way to reveal Heaven to us. The vision could be a loved one or a saint or our Blessed Mother or Christ Himself. God uses all these means to reveal to us that we are entering deeper into His mystical Life in us. Dreams, symbols, and visions help us to connect to Heaven in a more profound way. Does everyone have dreams, visions, or learn the symbolic voice of God? No. It all depends on how deep we dive into His Life. Picture a huge swimming pool. In the shallower part of the pool, the water would be three feet deep. Some people enter three feet of water. Some people like to enter deeper, so they dive in where the water is over their heads, where the water consumes their whole being. I like to dive deep into my prayer life in Jesus, and I respect others who are comfortable with standing in three feet of water. If we are dealing with those who dwell in the shallower waters, then we are to honor them where they are. If we who dive deep into the life of Christ were to pull the people in shallower water into the deeper water too quickly, they might feel that the water begins to choke them. If the water is over their heads, and they are not ready for such a deep prayer life, then they will feel like they are drowning instead of staying afloat where it seems peaceful and safe for them to rest and be refreshed in God. This process of entering the deeper water is a slow process, and we who are older in the Spirit must walk knowing how to help those who are beginning their journey in Jesus. It is in Christ's time, through the workings of the Holy Spirit, that all are brought deeper into the Life of Jesus. We need to cooperate with the Holy Spirit and honor one another where the Spirit of God has taken them instead of hindering them and making them feel intimidated in the life of God.

Doors That Are Christ…
All dwellings have a door and the door is Christ…

We cannot enter a deeper door into a deeper dwelling unless we enter into Christ as Christ is: Pure as the unblemished Lamb of God who takes away the sins of the world. As we do the turn around and begin to come down the mountain to serve the least of our brothers and sisters in dwellings three, two, and one, we have an easier time serving them. This is because the doors on these dwellings are now opened to us. We went through these dwellings and know what was expected of us. As we do the turn, we now know what is expected in our brothers and sisters who are in the third, second, and first dwelling. All those doors are now opened to us so that we can freely see what is blocking us from entering deeper into the life of Christ. Jesus told us that the more a person has, the more will be expected of him. God expects us to serve those who are in the shallower dwellings.

Padre Pio, a Mystical Saint …

It was said of him that he could read minds. What Padre Pio did was to see in his brothers and sisters what was blocking them. As they would come to confession, he knew what was blocking them, even if they themselves did not know. He could bring forth the sin he could see in them. The deeper we enter the mystical body of Christ, the deeper we see as Christ sees. This should give us all a boost to remain solid in Jesus. Our service will be more profound in the life we live in Jesus.

We see God's mystical life in the lives of all saints. I love to use Padre Pio's story because he lived his entire life in the perfection of Jesus. So many souls who came to Padre Pio for guidance were saved through his cooperation with Grace, which was extended to him from God to serve those who were lost.

Areas in us that need to increase in the third dwelling:

- Attachments to certain recited prayers. (Those who are in the third dwelling have a harder time praying from the heart. They are more comfortable with recited prayer.)

- Faithfulness to God

- Faithfulness to our Blessed Mother

- Faithfulness to our Holy Father the Pope

- Deep feelings of being persecuted. (Many times these souls are persecuted and misunderstood because God is chastening us from people who we want to impress such as a clergy or a nun. God chastises the ego from self-love to desiring to love Him above.)

- Being disowned by family and friends for changing our lives (They seem to think we have alienated them from our lives because we now find joy in God, our savior.)

- Chastisements from areas that keep us busy and pre-occupied. (God detaches areas in our lives that keep us busy and away from Him. He also is detaching us from areas that are not needed in our Divine Mission. We must attach to the areas that reflect His Divine Mission through us.)

- Moving in feelings because the senses are peaking. (God allows our senses to peak in this dwelling to bring us deeper into Heaven and to reveal His mysteries to us.)

- Experiences in the senses and great visions of Heavenly objects (Our senses are peaking in Jesus; we might see Him, smell Him, hear Him, touch Him, and taste Him. God uses our senses to strengthen us for the fourth dwelling.)

Areas in us that need to be purged in the third dwelling:

- Attachments to holy objects (A Sacramental is good, but when we use them to be seen by others to show how holy we are, they become blocks to God.)
- Attachments to private spiritual rituals (Two consecutive Masses a day.)
- Running from sinners instead of embracing them. (We need to help those who live in darkness to see the light of Christ in and through us.)
- Distrust of taking spiritual direction
- Arrogance in thinking we have arrived at the holiest we can become, and everyone needs to be where we are
- Wearing clothing to give the appearance that we are holy (We like people looking at us as though we are different. We might be thinking, "If I look holy, I must be holy.")
- Speaking on God's behalf without allowing the Spirit to speak. (We lack the ability to listen to God first and then to speak; this concept takes great discipline.)
- Getting stuck in the third dwelling from lack of spiritual direction
- Being misunderstood by many
- Feeling like we are all alone in the world, a victim soul
- Difficulty discerning God's way for our way (Instead of cooperating with the Holy Spirit, we begin to fight to remain in this dwelling because of the sweet peak of our senses in Him.)
- Losing the sweet sense of Him as we knew Him to be (Prayer might become hard for us to focus upon. Jesus is trying to numb the senses in us so we move deeper in Spirit.)
- A desire to stay in the third dwelling. (Begin to read the Bible more and ponder Him.)
- A need to discipline the flesh to dwell deeper in the Holy Spirit

In the first three dwellings of Purgatory, we must completely repent and reform, getting rid of anything that reflects evil or mortal sin that puts us back into original sin. Jesus sees how hard we have been working to get closer to Him and rewards us with deeper intimacy within Him.

Here is a list of virtuous actions that we can apply to deepen our lives in Christ Jesus:

- Take our Blessed Mother as our own Immaculate Mother. (Jesus gave her to us at the foot of the cross.)
- Avoid reflecting the unhealthy behavior of original sin to other people.
- Stop associating with people who live in the old behavior of sin where we once dwelled.
- Go to the Sacraments faithfully to be filled with Grace to become as holy as God is holy, pure as God is pure, innocent as God is innocent.
- Know the Sacraments are available for us to be filled with Grace.
- Start performing works of Mercy, both corporal and spiritual.
- Do everything out of Love for God.
- Read and ponder Scripture, applying it to our everyday lives and to the lives of others.
- Take time to listen to God speak to us.
- Take time to pray every day. Pray the rosary, novenas, or Stations of the Cross. Deep prayer is practiced by allowing ourselves to sit in the presence of God and allowing His presence to be entered into. We must deepen our awareness of being present and attentive to Him.
- Take time to adore our Lord in the Blessed Sacrament.
- Allow our Blessed Mother to guide us and instruct us on how to love her and her Son, Jesus Christ.
- Avoid becoming lazy in prayer.
- Place God first; ourselves second; others third.
- Enter prayer to be filled with Grace and to give others our virtuous life in Christ.
- Learn the Fruits and Gifts of God's life that are living in us so that we can grow in them and start to reflect them to others. This action takes a lot of self-control.

The Gifts of God's Life:

- Wisdom - To aspire to things that last forever

- Understanding – To enlighten our minds with the light of His truth

- Knowledge - To know, to love, and to serve God

- Counsel- To seek His kingdom first and choose to do God's will always

- Fortitude - To overcome evil and to endure our cross with strength for God

- Piety - To have peace and fulfillment in service to God

- Fear of the Lord - To have a loving reverence and a fear of offending the one we love, God

The Fruits of the Holy Spirit's Life:

- The Spirit of Love

- The Spirit of Joy

- The Spirit of Peace

- The Spirit of Patience

- The Spirit of Kindness

- The Spirit of Goodness

- The Spirit of Faithfulness

- The Spirit of Gentleness

- The Spirit of Self-Control

In each of the dwellings, we go into the garden of rest and try to rest with God as long as we can. The purer we become, the easier it will be to enter these gardens of intimacy in Jesus. These secret gardens in each dwelling are entered through the Spirit of God and are found deep inside us. When we enter into our secret garden, we enter with our eyes closed and in a relaxed position. The body will naturally begin to suspend itself as we enter deeper into the life of Jesus. His most Holy Spirit begins to breathe in us as we are breathing in Jesus. The sound of the breathing is very calming and we will naturally go deeper.

The goal in each of these secret gardens is to unite His Blessed Holy Spirit to our spirit where they become one. We enter deeper into the life of our Baptism, the life of Holy Trinity.

All first three dwellings concentrate more on the purging of the outside of the cup. This cup begins to become more internalized at the end of third dwelling.

This is where Jesus turns the water into wine. The water symbolizes the Holy Spirit. As the soul enters deeper into the life of the Holy Spirit, the Holy Spirit changes the water into wine to symbolize the deepening of the Spirit in us to the point of being in a state of intoxication in Spirit. The indwelling of our being is entering deeper and deeper and is becoming so attached to God's will that we lose any power of our own to move and begin to rest in His overwhelming glory. This glory overshadows us. This is why our Blessed Mother said, "Do everything Jesus tells us to do." At this point, she is leading us to her Son; it is here that Jesus transforms and unites our lives to His own. This union leaves us completely powerless. Our soul is melting in love with God. It is here where we are intoxicated with God's love, and He is embracing us as His own.

This is why when the Holy Spirit came on Pentecost Sunday, the Apostles looked drunk to others.

They were in a state of being detached from this world. They were in a suspension of the body and dwelling deep in God's Holy Spirit, the Fruit of the life of Christ Jesus, the choice wine.

✝✝✝

Spiritual Notes

Lamb of God
Who Takes Away the Sins of the World

The Fourth Dwelling of Purgatory

The fourth door opens: Jesus says, "Come Forward!"

The fourth dwelling is where the "crossover" takes place. It is here that we enter the Baptism of the fire of Spirit within us. It is here that the Spirit enters us in a more intimate way to purge the inside of the cup. This means our inner self must be purged to reflect the life of Christ living in us.

Baptism of Fire . . .
When we enter the fourth dwelling, we enter the baptism of fire. This baptism of fire purges everything deep within us that is not of God. These areas deep within us are areas that we sometimes repress because we do not want to deal with them. In the first, second, and third dwellings, the Baptismal waters washed our outside life and all that was dark within us. In the first three dwellings, Jesus teaches us how to live a holy life in obedience and, accordingly, to follow the Catholic Church and all Her Teachings. This life of holiness to which God calls us is little known by those who dwell in the flesh.

Now as we climb farther up the mountain of Baptism, Jesus calls us to enter into Him more intimately. He enters our interior to purge us with fire. This fire of purgation within us begins to remove all that is not of Him that has taken up its residence in us. This fire of purgation makes us feel like God has left us; for at this point in our growth, all we see is the fear and dysfunctional love that we might possess. Jesus needs us to be as pure as He is pure, so He allows us to see all that is in us that is not of Him. Instead of seeing and feeling Him as we did in the third dwelling, we lose our sense of Him so that our senses are turned inward. These senses allow us to see what is preventing us from seeing God deeper in our being. If God did not allow this to happen to us, we would not be able to rid ourselves of all that is in us that is not of Him. Thus, He must turn our eyes from experiencing Him for a short time, as we once did in the first, second, and third dwellings.

This fourth dwelling calls us to enter a deeper reason for following Jesus. The feelings of God that we experienced in the first three dwellings are now gone. This "turning in" to become perfect in the life of Jesus tells those who have come this far that the way they cooperated and followed Christ in the first three dwellings has become perfect. Now a new door in the Life of Christ has opened, and we enter deeper into His Life, a life that now needs us to follow Him in Faith…

Matthew 23: 23-29
Woe to you, scribes and Pharisees, you hypocrites. You cleanse the outside of the cup and dish, but inside they are full of plunder and self-indulgence. Blind Pharisee, cleanse first the inside of the cup, so that the outside also may be clean. Woe to you, scribes and Pharisees, you hypocrites. You are like whitewashed tombs, which appear beautiful on the outside, but inside are full of dead men's bones and every kind of filth. Even so, on the outside you appear righteous, but inside you are filled with hypocrisy and evildoing.

It is in this fourth dwelling that we enter the life of the Spirit. It is in this room that we experience His magnificent Light that purges us from all evil. In this dwelling, His light is so radiant that it makes us feel like we are in the dark. However, we are not. We are so exposed to His pure light of holiness that is showing not His divine face, but our face, and what we need to do to rid ourselves of all barriers that veil us from entering deeper into the beatific vision of His Divine face. In this fourth dwelling, we no longer see and feel with our natural senses. It is in this dwelling that we enter into a more profound Faith in Christ. This is where we enter into the Baptism of the Spirit who will purge us to sanctify us and bring us into the unblemished Lamb of God. It is here that we cross over and begin to dwell deeper in our Catholic Faith. We are filled with Sacramental Grace so that we can be sustained to withstand the purging from within and continue to walk forward in Christ' life in us.

This process seems foreign to us because we are accustomed to dwelling in feelings rather than in sheer faith. In these dwellings of purgation, we begin to see, through His illumination, our blocks or what is keeping us from entering into Him as He is. Some ignore this dwelling and become very arrogant and prideful, thinking God has left them to die in their sins.

God at this point seems distant, and some might think that He has abandoned them; on the contrary, He is purifying us of our sins by allowing us to see ourselves and what we have worshiped as false gods over the years and all that we brought into our temples that reflects Satan instead of our true image and likeness, Christ. This is how we have spent our inheritance on loose idols instead of remaining straight and strong in Jesus Christ. The Holy Spirit is purging us and completely bringing us into the holiness of God.

He is calling us to enter true love through the Spirit who is true Love and not some deceitful, pretentious, shallow way to love that fill our egos. He is calling us to become very pure in nature, God's nature. He is calling us to cleanse deep within us all that is not of Him and His image of holiness.

Some things we might see here are deep-rooted sins that come from wounds that lay dormant in us. These sins are the effects of original sin from dysfunctional behavior that might have been taught to us from childhood. Satan keeps us attached to dysfunctional ways, thinking we were loved, but the love that we might have experienced was not real love at all. It was dysfunctional, and it left us crippled and wounded as we grew up. As many of us grew, we grew in the shame of what was shown to us and we ended up repressing that wound and the shame attached to the dysfunction.

These areas do not always apply to our first parents. The dysfunctional area might have been afflicted on us by caretakers at school or children who taunted us. We learn improper behavior, behavior that is not the image or likeness of God, but takes on an image of original sin, which is Satan. A pagan lives in sin. If we are around pagans growing up, we learn dysfunctional behavior that reflects original sin. We lose our dignity in Christ and begin to dwell in and reflect original sin. We begin to lose our lives in Christ that we entered into on our Baptism day. Our robes become dirty, and the pure white that He robed us in begins to fade with veils of evil that cover our eyes and bring us into a deceitful life instead of remaining in truth. As the prodigal son takes his inheritance and squanders it, we do the same.

We take all the good Gifts and Fruits of God's life that He has filled us with on the day of our Baptism and squander them. His Divine Life in us is our true wealth inherited in Christ Jesus. Until we repent and reform by using the Sacrament of Reconciliation, we remain lost. Our robes, symbolizing our souls, remain filthy; our eyes are covered with veils of evil that leave us in confusion where Satan entraps us and isolates us in sin. We must remain consistent in the life Jesus is revealing to us; we must cooperate with the Holy Spirit and allow Him to purge us of all that is blocking our way up the mountain. We stand firm in our faith of Sacraments to keep us full of Grace so that we can withstand the purging process; Grace is what sustains us in the life of God because Grace is the life of God Himself. We must keep moving through these purging dwellings and not stop until we win the race and enter the seventh day of holiness. We must learn the Divine Plan of our Heavenly Father to enter into the narrow path of truth and the light of

41

life who is Christ. We must serve Him by making the turn to wash the feet of those who are in the shallower dwellings. This is the love that He expects us to live, for it is easy to love those who are easy to love. We need to serve Him by loving others, by bringing them into His fold, so that they too can know, love, and serve our Lord and enter Heaven, our true home in Christ Jesus.

We need to follow Christ as one body to enter our Father's house so that we can once again enter into the Divine Life of the Triune God who fills us with His divine life of Grace. Many souls never enter the fourth dwelling because they do not understand what God is doing here. It is very foreign from what they are accustomed to in the third dwelling because everything seemed so sweet and so holy in the third dwelling. God was filling us with visions and dreams of saints, strengthening us to enter this fourth dwelling. The fourth dwelling is where we walk by faith, not by those sweet feelings of being holy. We enter the holiness of God by the purging fire within us. Our natural senses seem to be dead, and many think Jesus has left them. The storms in our life seem to rise, and we begin to see in us what needs to be purified. Jesus leaves us here until we cooperate with the Holy Spirit and help Him purge us of everything that we have brought into our lives that is not of our faith. Here is where the apostles were in the boat, and Jesus was sleeping by the stern on a pillow. The apostles saw the raging waters start to enter the boat, and they began to be afraid, so they woke Jesus up. Jesus calmed the storm and looked at them and said, "You with little faith." In this fourth dwelling, we must stand on the rock of our Catholic faith and cooperate with the Holy Spirit who is purging the inside of our cups to stand straight and strong in the life of the Sacraments. This life of faith is filled with Grace, Grace that will sustain us through all the storms in our lives that will appear in this fourth dwelling. The Holy Spirit brings us into the fourth dwelling where we need to learn in Christ what He is doing through the purgation process, and so it is that the inside of us must be purified.

Matthew 3:10-17
When John realized that a lot of Pharisees and Sadducees were showing up for a baptismal experience because it was becoming the popular thing to do, he exploded: "Brood of snakes! What do you think you're doing slithering down here to the river? Do you think a little water on your snake skins is going to make any difference? It's your life that must change, not your skin! And don't think you can pull rank by claiming Abraham as father. Being a descendant of Abraham is neither here nor there. Descendants of Abraham are a dime a dozen. What counts is your life. Is it green and blossoming? Because if it's deadwood, it goes on the fire. "I'm baptizing you here in the river, turning your old life in for a kingdom life.

Here we see John the baptizer bringing up truth in the Pharisees and Sadducees. It is the same truth for all of us who live life in the spirit of being obtuse. We are growing, and God does not want us to clean just the outside of our cups or our being. We need to enter a more interior Baptism. The Holy Spirit will ignite the kingdom of life within us, transforming us through the fire of Baptism to bring us deeper into our union in Christ.

He is going to clean house, making a clean sweep of our lives. He will place everything that is truth in its proper place before God; everything false he will put out with the trash to be burned.

Here we see how we must clean our interior temples. This fourth dwelling is bringing us deeper into the Holy Spirit's mission of sanctifier to purge us with the fire of all that is not of God.

Matthew 3:13-17
Jesus then appeared, arriving at the Jordan River from Galilee. He wanted John to baptize him, but John objected, saying, "I'm the one who needs to be baptized, not you!" Nevertheless, Jesus insisted. The moment Jesus came out of the Baptismal waters, the skies opened up and he saw God's Spirit—it looked like a dove—descending and landing on him. Along with the Spirit, a voice said, "This is my Son, chosen and marked by my love, delight of my life."

The life we enter in Baptism is the life of Christ Jesus. Therefore, what Jesus does in Scripture is what we need to do to follow Him. Jesus did not need to be baptized; He is the Baptism. He showed us what to do to follow Him into the Kingdom.

When we are baptized in the waters of Christ Jesus, the entire life of Jesus enters into our soul, making a home within us: Father, Son, and Holy Spirit. The whole Trinitarian Life of God is now making His home within us. For us to begin to decrease, we must enter this fourth dwelling and allow Christ to increase. When we enter this fourth dwelling, we begin to think we have lost our way or that the way is dry, but the lost feeling we are experiencing here is the foreignness of this dwelling. It is not of flesh and blood as we once knew life in Christ to be in the third dwelling. It is of Spirit. Here is where we enter the purging life of His fire. What we will begin to experience in the fourth dwelling is a complete change from the water that once quenched us in the third dwelling to a place that seems painfully dry.

Many of us call this area of our prayer life "dry prayer" or "the darkness" or "the dryness." It is not dark at all; it is so enlightened it blinds us to what was in the third dwelling, life lived in the flesh. The light is the fire that will purge us of all the wounds and sins that lay deep within us that we have repressed over our entire lifetime.

I call this area "the sea of turbulence" because it is here that this seemingly dry prayer is not dry at all; it is the story of Jesus in the boat with His Apostles. Jesus is resting in the stern on a pillow while the storm is beginning to affect the boat, and the Apostles begin to cry out to Jesus, "Don't you care about what is happening to us with this storm?"

The fourth dwelling is the crossover. We keep hearing in Scriptures how Jesus got into the boat and crossed over. When we cross over to the other side from flesh into Spirit, we are not accustomed to this life of Spirit. In the third dwelling, we were accustomed to praying in our physical way, with many recited words.

In this fourth dwelling, we not only enter deeper into our interior beings in Christ, we enter deeper into prayer. The prayer that we enter in the fourth dwelling is praying with words that are attached to our hearts, and the fruit of this prayer is clear truth, truth that needs to be expressed to God that reveals in us the areas where we hurt.

God is calling us to enter deeper into His most Blessed Spirit to pray in spirit and truth. Every time I say "truth" in my writings, I am speaking of the Holy Spirit. Therefore, the Holy Spirit, who is all truth, brings us deeper into the prayer that is Jesus, the one who delivers us from sin.

The dryness that we might think is here is summed up as the lack of feeling God, as we once did in the third dwelling. The dryness we might think we are experiencing here is the decreasing from what was in the first three dwellings that kept us attached to our old dysfunctional ways. This decreasing of our dysfunctional ways is a dying of the old self, and the increasing in functional love is a continuous new birth experience of entering deeper into the life of the Blessed Trinity.

In this fourth dwelling, our senses are numbed so that we will enter deeper within ourselves to find God. However, in looking for God deep within, we find nothing but issues of pain that we did not want to deal with growing up. It is here in this fourth dwelling that God begins to reveal the inner issues in us that need to be purified. He is crossing us over into the fire of spirit to bring us deeper into His image and likeness that we entered in Baptism. Much of what we will experience in the fourth dwelling will allow us to see what is holding us back from entering our Baptismal life.

Jesus is the divine teacher who brings us into His mystical life. The Holy Spirit is the divine person who sanctifies and purifies to prepare us to enter into Jesus so that Jesus can deliver us into Abba to rest in all of His goodness. What we once hid from in the first, second, and third dwellings begins to reveal itself in this fourth dwelling. It seems like a storm that will not calm down. This storm begins the life of the Holy Spirit and the fire of purging from within us all that is not of the true image and likeness of Christ that we inherited in Baptism.

What we need to do in this dwelling is to cooperate with the Spirit of God to purge us. We do not need to hide any more. We do not need to be ashamed of what is hidden deep within us. We have healing Sacraments to help us be restored and healed through Grace. This is our Eucharistic life in Christ Jesus. We never leave Mass and all that takes place at Mass. Every ounce of Scripture, every ounce of us, is at Mass every moment of the day. Jesus, being all Wisdom, had to compact Mass the night the soldiers were coming to take Him away. The mission of His deliverance at Mass is the same deliverance that He is taking us through in these dwellings.

In this fourth dwelling, when we go to pray, our desire is to enter peace and joy with great solitude. This is what we desire in God because God is peace and complete joy. He does give great solitude, but not in the next two dwellings. Our prayer here seems dry because God is not filling our desired need of peace, joy, and solitude in Him.

His desire for us in this dwelling is the storm. We must remember the Apostles in the boat during the storm when Jesus was resting in the stern on the pillow, and nothing was disturbing Him. The Apostles were upset about seeing the storm and the effects it was taking on them; however, Jesus did not leave them there to die. He addressed the storm. Jesus is with us in the storm, and the Holy Spirit is showing us what needs to be addressed in this dwelling so that we, too, can rest on that same pillow in the stern in union with Jesus.

What lesson did the Apostles need to learn in this passage of Scripture? To live in faith, God never leaves us. We need to grow in faith, which is our Catholic way of seeing Him. Let us go farther in this dwelling. In this dwelling, we begin to see what bothers us rather than experiencing the sweetness of God. These areas of pain that rise up in us when we are at prayer are the areas God is showing us that we need to address. When we enter prayer and we begin to see these areas that are painful, know that these are the areas where the Holy Spirit is stirring within us so that we begin to see what we have repressed that is not of God and all of His goodness. These areas have to be dealt with, and the only way to rid ourselves of them is to deal with them. The beatific vision is to be face to face with God. In these next two dwellings, God brings us face to face with what is in us that is not of His life. We must confront these areas to rid ourselves of them and to enter a more interior union in Christ. This purifying process might take years to get through. The faster we see what God is showing us and the faster we deal with it completely, the faster we will get through this dwelling. These pain-filled areas in us are sometimes very deep; they are determined by how deeply we were wounded as we grew in a life that was not of God, but of original sin. All that we learned and all our behavior in the false life of worldly gain disfigured us as we grew in our Earthly life. When people grow in a dysfunctional way, not knowing God in their lives, they tend to pursue false gods to fill their pain-filled areas. They fill these areas of pain with ways that heighten their egos. These areas are power, lust, and greed, and these false areas need to be purged. We need to re-enter our Baptismal inheritance and detach from all the evil ways that kept us away from God. We need to be brought back into the image and likeness of Christ. The storm will never be quiet and be at peace if we do not address what disfigured us. Jesus addressed the storm, so we need to follow Him and address the storms in our lives, also.

When we pray but problems keep surfacing. Here are some examples of what storms might be rising:

- Our relationship with our spouse might become distant. This sometimes happens because we now are deeper in the life of God, and perhaps our spouse has not yet converted back to God.

- If we are in Holy Orders, our position as priests might seem to be dry and lonely, making us feel isolated. The Holy Spirit at this point is showing us deep within ourselves what areas need to be purified. These areas become our focal point, and through this realization, the way becomes trying and painful.

When in prayer, listen to what the Holy Spirit is trying to tell us. He will begin to bring up within us all that needs purifying. He needs us to cooperate with Him so that this dryness will end, and our lives in Him will be able to reflect more of His glory. If we co-operate with the Holy Spirit, our prayer life will return, and it will be more peaceful and enjoyable. The distractions will end because we begin to cooperate with the Holy Spirit to rid ourselves of everything that is not of Christ.

In this dwelling, listen to the distractions. They are the storm, and we need to address them as Christ did. Every reading in the Bible where He is doing something or saying something, Jesus is revealing these dwellings of purgation and what needs to be done for us to enter Him more deeply. The purging stops when we enter the seventh dwelling where we rest from all the work of the storms that we have repressed. We pretended to be resting on the pillow, but we were not there yet. Pretending in life reflects Satan. He is the great pretender who tries to copy God, yet always comes short. He tempts and tests us; that is all the power he has. Even temptation is used for the glory of God Himself. Amen…

Now let us go a step deeper. When we take the time to go into the storm and rely on the Holy Spirit to keep us afloat, we keep our eyes fixed on Christ Jesus who will not allow us to sink; instead, we will walk on the stormy waters. This is not a time to change our vocations or run away from the pain of what He is showing us. We must trust Him here. He is showing us what needs to be attended to in our lives so that when this area is resolved and the pain does not affect us any more, we will be able to rest in Him more deeply. This is why I call the seventh dwelling "the seventh day." In each dwelling is the garden of rest. We enter this garden of rest when we have listened to the Spirit of God and have dealt with the storm that He is allowing us to experience. Once we begin to deal with it, He is right there waiting to hold us. The holding will not be long, at least for some of us, because there is more work to be done, and He does not want us to be sidetracked where we once rested in the third dwelling. He does not want us to go backwards; therefore, He does not let us rest long. Here is where we need to trust Him, not with our feelings but with faith. We must remain steadfast in the Sacraments and go to confession when we see a flashback that is shaming us of what once took place so that we can remove the shame and be pure in the image and likeness of Jesus as the Lamb of God.

"Prayer of rest" is only experienced when we cooperate with the Holy Spirit in the areas in us that are not at rest. Once we eliminate all these areas, we naturally enter "prayer of rest." When Jesus asked Peter, "Who do you say that I am?", Peter said, "You are the Christ." Peter received this truth not from flesh or blood, but from his intimate prayer life in God. Jesus was very proud of Peter, and because of being the first Apostle to enter His revelation in truth, Jesus gave Peter the keys to Heaven as our first Pope. Jesus then held Peter in this great embrace of Peter's pure understanding of who Jesus was. Peter quickly went back into what felt right and responded to Jesus, "We don't have to suffer and die." Do we see how quickly Jesus held Peter in this elevated dwelling? Jesus response was, "Get behind me, Satan." The holding did not last long because Peter wanted to go back and dwell on what he thought was holy. Jesus was telling Peter and the other Apostles what needed to be done to take away the sins of the world, but they thought that this kind of pain did not have to be experienced. We want so desperately to glorify ourselves instead of glorifying God.

We cannot glorify God or enter into His glory if we remain in our fallen image. Our fallen image needs to be cleansed. We need to be purified and sanctified so that we can enter our true image and likeness of Christ and be pleasing to God and enter Heaven forever.

Eucharist . . .
John 6: 54-58
Whoever eats my flesh and drinks my blood has eternal life, and I will raise him on the last day. For my flesh is true food, and my blood is true drink. Whoever eats my flesh and drinks my blood remains in me and I in him. Just as the living Father sent me and I have life because of the Father, so also the one who feeds on me will have life because of me. This is the bread that came down from heaven. Unlike your ancestors who ate and still died, whoever eats this bread will live forever."

It is in this dwelling that we must walk and stand in great faith. So many are afraid to enter deeper into the darkness of faith. The faith here is darkened so that we see in us what needs to be purged. It is in this fourth dwelling that we are becoming very Blessed. I will try to explain it in this way: When we entered dwelling one, two, and three, we were always looking at the light of Christ. *O, the light is so beautiful, I see the light, and the light is Christ* (St. Paul's conversion). The light is warm and cozy, and it makes us feel so special. However, in dwellings one, two, and three, we, at this point, are looking at the light as if we were in one room and Jesus was in another, divided by a glass. We, on our side, are always looking through the glass and seeing this magnificent light.

When we enter the fourth dwelling, we enter into the same room as Jesus; we enter into the magnificent light. This is a big difference. The light is so brilliant that it blinds us to the face of Christ or what we, through our senses, thought was the face of Christ. It is in this fourth dwelling that we must start to see Jesus through the face of peace. Peace is His gift to us. For peace is Jesus Himself. It is in this dwelling that we become very blessed. It is the same state used to canonize a saint, but in this case, Jesus Himself is calling us into His blessed life. How great is this? We are so precious to Him in this fourth dwelling that He has embraced us for Himself for all of eternity if we stay with Him.

Many souls in this fourth dwelling still crave the third dwelling, which filled them with such greatness because the fourth dwelling is so foreign to them. Many souls become stuck and think Jesus has left them in this fourth dwelling. Our senses are now darkened. Jesus does not want us to walk in Him with feelings. He is calling us to enter His life with faith. We are at the door of great faith. Enter and allow the Holy Spirit to purge all the things that are in us that keep us from entering Jesus deeper. Does this take much faith? Yes …! It is in faith that virtue is made perfect. He is bringing us into His perfect life. He keeps us sanctified to enter our sainthood in Him.

Our prayer life in this fourth dwelling will change. Many distractions will occur. We might want to say the rosary or the Stations of the Cross, and our minds may keep wandering. God is calling us into a deeper prayer now. We begin to enter the silence and the stillness of being with Him, but again it takes great faith to know God has not left us. He is showing us that He is God and wants very much to teach us through this prayer of stillness and silence that we are sharing in the great mysteries of His magnificent Divine Life. It is in this stillness that Jesus begins to commune with us if we listen to Him.

We are not crazy. We are entering the deepest dwellings in His most intimate embrace, and He wants to share with us all of the good of creation. Remember this:

On the sixth day, God was finished with all that He created, and on the seventh day, He looked at all that He created and rested. This wonderful fourth dwelling is where God begins to show what is blocking us from Him. It is in this fourth dwelling that God wants us to use the Blessed Sacraments to remain in Him in all of perfection, the same way we began our new life in Him in our Baptism. Sacraments are given to us in Christ to stay sanctified in the life we already have in Him that we entered through Baptism. Sacraments are what we need to cling to. It is in the Sacraments that we begin to dwell in deeper faith because the Sacraments are what we believe in. By living in the Sacraments, we enter faith at a much deeper level.

I am not saying this fourth dwelling will be easy. It has many areas that are demanding and painful. God allows trials of this magnitude so that we become strong in His Grace and do not collapse into distress. Our desire for outside holiness seems to be gone; many believe God has left them. This dwelling seems dry and not pleasurable at all. The souls who enter here think God has abandoned them, but in all honesty, He is holding them closer to Him now than before because they are nearer to Him.

The Effect of the Discourse
John 6: 62-64
After hearing his words, many of his disciples remarked, "This sort of talk is hard to endure! How can anyone take it seriously?" Jesus was fully aware that his disciples were murmuring in protest at what he had said. "Does it shake your faith?" he asked them. "What, then if we were to see the Son of Man ascends to where he was before…? It is the spirit that gives life; the flesh is useless. The words I spoke to you are spirit and

life. Yet among you there are some who do not believe…. This is why I have told you that no one can come to me unless it is granted him by the Father."

The fire of purgation is very purging in the fourth dwelling. God wants us now more than we want Him. He knows we have worked very hard to this point to become pure for Him in Christ. (When Jesus came out of the River Jordan, a voice from the Heavens said, "This is my beloved Son, in whom I am well pleased.") We enter the Baptism of the Holy Spirit now. We no longer are washing the flesh to make room for the Spirit; it is the Spirit purging us with fire to enter His life through spirit. We enter a deeper, more glorified life through the Spirit of truth. To bring us into truth, we must face truth.

The trials that we endure for the sake of His kingdom make us strong so that we can endure and help others to pick up their crosses, too. We can now keep following Jesus into Heaven.

Romans 8: 4-11
For if we have grown into union with Him through a death like His, we shall also be united with Him in the resurrection. We know that our old self was crucified with Him, so that our sinful body might be done away with, that we might no longer be in slavery to sin. For the concern of the flesh is hostility toward God; it does not submit to the law of God, nor can it; and those who are in the flesh cannot please God. But you are not in the flesh; on the contrary, you are in the spirit, if only the Spirit of God dwells in you. Whoever does not have the Spirit of Christ does not belong to him. But if Christ is in you, although the body is dead because of sin, the spirit is alive because of righteousness. If the Spirit of the one who raised Jesus from the dead dwells in you, the one who raised Christ from the dead will give life to your mortal bodies also, through his Spirit that dwells in you.

Throughout the dwellings, Jesus is bringing us into a life of greater Faith

Rubber Band Effect . . .
In the fourth dwelling, many souls feel like they have a rubber band around them, keeping them bound and not allowing them to feel free in serving God the way they would like to serve Him. Jesus needs us to remain faithful to Him and to know that He is still schooling us in His Life. So in the fourth and fifth dwellings, we feel this rubber band effect on us. It begins in the fourth dwelling and becomes even tighter in the fifth dwelling. Our desire is to be free of all that binds us to Earth so that we can freely serve Him as we wish. His desire is still for us to be schooled in Him. By living in faith in Him, we

learn how to endure the trials and tribulations that attach to us in the life in Christ, and we become even stronger through them.

Again in these dwellings, God is bringing us into a deeper faith. Faith is not something we see. It is when we remain in faith that our lives in Jesus grow. This cooperation in faith leads us into our Divine Mission in Christ.

Remember, *the trials of the just will be many. Also, it is through suffering that we enter the salvation of Christ Himself* ...

It is in these two short sentences from the Scriptures that we find our home in Christ.

Areas in us that need to increase in the fourth dwelling:

- Flashes of past abuse or pain-filled memories of our younger years that left us wounded. (Take these flashes to the confessional. This is the Holy Spirit illuminating us into helping Him purge us. We are entering a deeper dwelling of purity.)
- A loss of Jesus as we once knew Him through the senses, yet He is closer to us and He is deepening our faith through the illumination we are entering
- Greater faith by not allowing our old feelings to surface
- Abandonment from friends and loved ones who do not follow their faith
- Lack of fitting in with others
- A sense of dry prayer (This prayer is purifying us so that we can cooperate with the Holy Spirit.)
- A lack of understanding from others (God is chastising us.)
- God chastising the things we once enjoyed (God chastises us to bring us higher up the mountain to the point of our life's mission.)
- A pulling away from volunteering in every area as we did in the first three dwellings (The volunteering needs to be brought more profoundly into God's predestined mission for us in our sanctified lives in Him.)
- More intimacy with Jesus (This intimacy is more of a great longing.)
- A deeper need to trust Jesus (He needs us to trust Him so that He can bring us deeper into faith and away from feelings.)
- Detachment from the objects that we once thought were so important
- Detachment from infatuations with those who represent holiness
- Becoming more attached to the Sacraments and God Himself

- A desire to do God's will (We must decrease the desire of doing our own will. We are being purified like gold in fire. The end result is complete joy forever with God!)

- Dreams that bring up what might be blocking us from entering deeper into the life of Christ

- Dreams that direct us into the area we need to go to enter deeper and to fulfill God's will in our lives

- Dreams that encourage us in our lives in Jesus so that we do not lose hope and fall back

- Cooperating with the Holy Spirit in being purged to enter deeper into the purity of God's life in us (These are the dwellings He takes us through.)

- Praying with loved ones

- A desire to share our lives in God with others

- Ridding ourselves of inhibitions (They must be eradicated for us to be free to do God's work.)

- Seeing our wounds and trying to heal them through the healing Sacraments

- Beginning to see how the cup needs to be purified inside, not just outside (God is internalizing and deepening the purifying deep within us to bring us into His holiness.)

- A deeper desire to help bring others to know, love, and serve our Lord

- A tremendous dryness in acts as well as prayer (God is showing us what needs to be purged in us. Listen to Him and follow His teachings.)

- Desires to see and develop our special Gifts in God

- Knowing God more completely to serve Him in others

- Listening to our spiritual directors (Find a mature spiritual director who knows these dwellings and can guide us through them.)

Areas in us that need to be purged in the fourth dwelling:

- Fear of being in deep sin when we are not (Many times, we begin showing signs of obsessive-compulsive disorder, doing activities over and over to get them perfect. For example, we might say the rosary repeatedly until we say it perfectly, or we might recite prayers daily, thinking that if we do not recite these prayers today, we will not be praying perfectly as we should be.)

- A feeling of pretending to pray, instead of really praying
- Detachments from commitments because of a lack of feeling connected
- Sadness and loneliness (These feelings are the detachments of the third dwelling. He needs us to walk in great faith here.)
- Feelings and emotions that are trying to lead us to awaken our senses again (We need to discipline our desire to jump from the third dwelling that felt good to the fourth dwelling where God is calling us into deeper faith.)
- Detachment of ego from filling up the senses
- Going off the path to find Him in other ways, maybe leaving our faith to venture off to find more fellowship
- Rebellion against teachings of the Church (No respect for fellow clergy.)
- Lack of reverence when in Church
- Illusions by the devil (Satan uses these illusions to keep us trapped so that we do not proceed further in the dwellings. Many souls remain in these illusions because they refuse to see truth.)

When entering into these dwellings, many walk in degrees of feelings, reason, and faith. The way we walk through these dwellings reveal where we are in them. In the first three dwellings, these souls walk through life being led more by their feelings. They walk in what feels good to them, and God uses their natural lives through the senses to lead them forth. In the fourth and fifth dwellings, these souls walk by using their reason. They use the intellect to connect to God and others. You can hear them when they speak everything is out of a book.

In the sixth and seventh dwelling, these souls walk in great faith first. It is not that they do not feel or use their emotional body they do but it does not lead them. It is not that they do not use the intellect to connect to God and others, they do but it does not lead them, faith leads them and they are always looking for the hand of God to lead them in all areas.

Spiritual Notes

Lamb of God
Who Takes Away the Sins of the World

The Fifth Dwelling of Purgatory:

The fifth door opens: Jesus says, "Come Forward!"

When we enter the fifth dwelling many childhood wounds are brought up within us and we begin to see the effects that these wounds had on us. These effects and the pain from our wounds are what a lot of us are reflecting. Jesus wants us to reflect His light of glory so that others will see the light and come forth from the darkness where they dwell. If we reflect these areas in us that are wounded, we will not be able to cooperate with Jesus by reflecting His light. These wounded areas deep within us have to be healed, not only the wound but also the effect of the wound that we have lived with for many years. The effects of these wounds are what keep us bond to the wound. The rubber band effect I talked about in the fourth dwelling is even tighter now and many feel frustrated and discouraged in their journey in Christ. It is in this fifth dwelling that Abba needs you to trust Jesus with all you heart, not only Jesus, but the workings of the Holy Spirit who is the Divine Person who is purging and sanctifying you through bringing up these wounded areas and the effects the wounds took on you. Continue to walk in deep faith and do not abandon your prayer life, and know that this too will pass when all the wounds and the effects of the wounds are healed.

Knowledge of Discernment . . .
In this dwelling, the Holy Spirit is bringing us deeper into knowledge. I will call this the "knowledge of discerning." The knowledge of discerning is for us to understand that the events that might have happened to us when we were young filled us with false love. This false love wounded us deep within. Children are innocent love; they believe what they learn, and they take in what they observe. Many of us come from abusive backgrounds. This abuse might have been in our homes through dysfunctional parents or siblings or at a caretaker's home or a relative's home. Also, many children are tormented when they go

to school by other children who make fun of them and abuse them. All the ways that our innocence has been wounded are what our Lord wants us to see in this fifth dwelling. It is not that God is reminding us of these wounds to hurt us all over again. He wants us to see them so that we can discern between what is real love and what is false love. We feel like we are in great darkness. On the contrary, He has us illuminated in Him in this fifth dwelling so that we can see into the darkness of the wounds and understand how these abusive wounds affected us.

This abuse affects us in the deepest part of our being, and the effects of the abuse wound our innocence in the life we live in Christ Jesus. It is like someone who robs children of their innocence, making them think that the abusive treatment that went along with the robbery of innocence is the right way to reach out to love us, when all along, it is wounding us and affecting us deep within. The child that is wounded becomes confused about knowing what real love is, and then begins to grow with a defect of not knowing God for who God is, real Love. This defect hinders the child from knowing God as a loving Lord, so the wound is not only hindering the person in God, it is hindering God from being one with the person. God in this fifth dwelling allows us to enter the pain of our wounds. We can then discern what real love is and come back to Him without being hindered by the false love that confused our knowledge of God as a loving Abba.

This process is very pain-filled and sometimes may take years to heal. Some are affected more than others, and if the pain from the wound is too deep, they might begin to pick up vices to numb the pain. Then they have more issues on top of deeper issues. Jesus cares more about the wound and healing it from within. He will bring us to the wound first and the pain it creates within us in this fifth dwelling. When the wound is healed and the pain subsides, he will bring us to the vice that we might have picked up to numb the wound. These vices are false ways of numbing the pain of the wound. The wound and the vice have to be completely healed in us. Usually when the wound heals completely, the vice will naturally end by our desire to give it up.

Jesus needs us to know without a shadow of a doubt that God's love is not trickery. He is solid Love, because He is all Love. These wounds of abuse or dysfunctional behavior that we learn are often repeated and passed down to other innocent victims. We want to stop the abuse before other innocent people suffer from the same wounds and pain that we experienced. Passing on learned, abusive behavior must stop through the Grace of God that lives within us. This process takes much discipline and cooperation.

When we enter this fifth dwelling and see in us these dark wounds and how they affected us and how we might have affected others by them, we need to cooperate with the purging of the Spirit to allow ourselves to be healed. This purification that leads us deeper into the Life of God allows us to realize God, and who He really is. He is a solid Love that can be trusted; He will never trick us into demeaning our innocence in Him.

When the Lord brings us here in this fifth dwelling to purify our wounds and the pain that surfaces from them, many people need counseling. I sometimes suggest the Sacrament of Anointing. I also suggest that we bring with us to confession the person who created the abuse so that we can ask for Grace to forgive the person or persons. If we hold on to the anger and the revenge that we might be feeling for the person or the persons, then we are holding on to the abuse. For our healing process and for theirs, we must let go completely. Jesus has asked us not to hold anyone bound in sin, We must forgive completely so that we are not held in the pain ourselves. This process is a slow process. It might take years to see all the areas where we were affected and wounded.

We will know we are healed in many different areas of our lives. One of those areas is that the thought of the abuse does not affect us anymore. We have given up our vice to numb the pain of the abuse. We have peace and joy in our lives. We will see in our emotional behavior that we can take correction without defending ourselves all the time. In our prayer life, we will enter periods of tremendous peace. We have fewer distractions, if any. We begin to hear the voice of God directing us in different ways. In Scripture, some of those ways are in listening to others speak and then hearing God speak to correct those who are speaking to us. He will embrace us when we least expect it. All these wonderful moments with Him are His ways of letting us know how happy He is with us in the way we have cooperated with the Holy Spirit. He will embrace us for all that we went through to enter His fullness of Love.

Cooperating in This Process of His Purging Love . . .
This purging process is very hard for the person who enters the fifth dwelling. If we cooperate with the purging process through the workings of the Holy Spirit, the time in this state is brief. Many souls do not understand this dwelling when they enter. They remain for years in this state because they become stuck in the pain that this abuse has left in the soul.

This pain seems to overwhelm people, bringing them into even greater darkness; this darkness of misery brings them into deep depression. The healing process is to go into the wound and use the means Jesus has instituted for us to be healed as quickly as we can. Sacraments heal in a divine way, so we should receive the Sacraments often. A good spiritual guide or director is advisable, one who knows what God is doing to help the person get through this fifth dwelling in the most cooperative, quick way. A good spiritual director guides us through the Holy Spirit and all that He is doing within us to bring us into full health who is Christ.

Mother Theresa went through this misery for years. When we read her writings, we can understand how she felt God left her. Faith here, in this fifth dwelling, becomes almost unbearable, and those who endure to the end will reap His benefits. A good spiritual director who knows these purging dwellings will be the best guide for those who follow Christ and enter this far.

Heb.10: 30-39
We know the one who said: "Vengeance is mine; I will repay," and again: "The Lord will judge his people." It is a fearful thing to fall into the hands of the living God. Remember the days past when, after you had been enlightened, you endured a great contest of suffering. At times you were publicly exposed to abuse and affliction; at other times we associated ourselves with those so treated. We even joined in the sufferings of those in prison and joyfully accepted the confiscation of our property, knowing that we had a better and lasting possession. Therefore, do not throw away our confidence; it will have great recompense. We need endurance to do the will of God and receive what he has promised. "For, after a brief moment, he who is to come shall come; he shall not delay. But my one shall live by faith, and if he draws back I take no pleasure in him." We are not among those who draw back and perish, but among those who have faith and will possess life. But my one shall live by faith, and if he draws back I take no pleasure in him." We are not among those who draw back and perish, but among those who have faith and will possess life. Therefore, since we are surrounded by so great a cloud of witnesses, let us rid ourselves of every burden and sin that clings to us and persevere in running the race that lies before us

Heb. 12: 1-14
Therefore, since we are surrounded by so great a cloud of witnesses, let us rid ourselves of every burden and sin that clings to us and persevere in running the race that lies before us while keeping our eyes fixed on Jesus, the leader and perfecter of faith. For the sake of the joy that lay before him he endured the cross, despising its shame, and has taken his seat at the right of the throne of God. Consider how he endured such opposition from sinners, in order that we may not grow weary and lose heart. In your struggle against sin we have not yet resisted to the point of shedding blood. We have also forgotten the exhortation addressed to we as sons: "My son, do not disdain the discipline of the Lord or lose heart when reproved by him; for whom the Lord loves, he disciplines; he scourges every son he acknowledges." Endure your trials as "discipline"; God treats us as sons. For what "son" is there whom his father does

not discipline? If we are without discipline, in which all have shared, we are not sons but bastards. Besides this, we have had our Earthly fathers to discipline us, and we respected them. Should we not (then) submit all the more to the Father of spirits and live? They disciplined us for a short time as seemed right to them, but he does so for our benefit, in order that we may share his holiness. At the time, all discipline seems a cause not for joy but for pain, yet later it brings the peaceful fruit of righteousness to those who are trained by it. So strengthen your drooping hands and your weak knees. Make straight paths for your feet, that what is lame may not be dislocated.

The Holy Spirit is stripping us of all that is left over from the old life of learned dysfunctional sin and behavior that left us wounded. This dwelling is the deepest of all dwellings that purge what has been repressed for so long. These wounds are very deep; the wounds and the memory of them need to be exposed so that we can take a closer look at them. For years, many of us have been repressing these wounds of dysfunction. Maybe we repressed them so we would not blame anyone, or maybe we repressed them because they were too painful. It is in this fifth dwelling that we must go into the wound and see what effects it is having on us.

Many of our inhibitions come from these wounds. Unless these wounds are healed, we will still walk in our old inhibitions that keep us bound to our old lives of sin. God wants us to go into the wound and see the effects that the wound had on our behavior. When we begin to deal with the pain deep within us and allow the emotion that is attached to the wound to surface, we begin to deal with much emotion that was repressed. When we deal with the wound, we even begin to see how we begin to dream. Many people who say they never dream have repressed so much of the pain of these wounds that they have not allowed themselves to enter into any emotion, If they did, they would bring up the pain of the wound. This fifth dwelling is where the Holy Spirit begins bringing up past issues that reveal these wounds. He needs us to go into the wounded area and deal with the effects to be healed. Once we deal with the wounds and their effects, the wounds and the pain are healed, allowing us to enter deeper into the life of Christ.

Illusions
Many who have repressed wounds have also repressed their emotions because of the pain it would bring up within them. The outcome of this behavior is living a life of illusions. These illusions-suppress the truth of the wounded area. The illusions keep us bound to fantasy rather than living in truth. Once we begin to deal with the wound and the pain deep within us, the falseness of the illusions begin to subside. The illusions that once kept us caught in falsehood begin to disappear, and we enter deeper into truth. His truth leads us into living every moment in the presence of God Himself.

Our Prayer Life in the Fifth Dwelling

It is at the end of this fifth dwelling that our prayer life begins to return to being peaceful and very fruitful in Jesus. Our intimacy is growing deeper in Christ, and this relationship seems to be more of a loving one-on-one relationship.

Many souls are praying and talking to God all day long, even waking up in the middle of the night to be with Him. Many flashbacks are still occurring to remind us of areas that still need to be addressed. Our commitment in Christ at this point is very solid. It is not that we cannot leave Him; it is that there is no other place on all of the Earth that could fill us as He is now filling us. We are on our way to entering into the sixth dwelling.

At the end of this fifth dwelling, the rubber band that once was so tightly holding us back from entering into our mission in serving Him begins to loosen. We now are much more schooled in the life of Jesus. He needs us to teach others, so we begin to see our mission in Christ. He begins to bring us farther up the mountain of transfiguration to reflect His glory on Earth as it is in Heaven

Areas in us that need to increase in the fifth dwelling:

- The surfacing of many wounds and the effects of the wounds
- Ridding ourselves of illusions that keep us bound to falsehood
- Feelings of being trapped and unable to enter our specific mission to serve Jesus (We feel like we are in a rubber band effect that influences our desire to serve Him, yet we still need to be schooled in His Life.)
- Removal of the emptiness in our lives (God seems to be in us, but He seems to be resting and not caring about our trials and tribulations. He is teaching us deeper faith in Him.)
- Allowing God to teach us how to pray by resting in us as He wants us to rest in Him through all the trials and tribulations
- Beginning to have a stronger communing with God instead of abandoning prayer
- A deeper desire to serve God in doing our corporal and spiritual works of mercy
- Strength obtained from the many trials and tribulations we are now encountering
- Cooperation with God instead of fighting against Him
- A desire is to be very pure for God
- A desire to receive the Sacraments frequently to be as pure as God is pure

- Rejection of clergy that might misunderstand us (The clergy might see in us the holiness of God, but if they are not practicing their faith as they should or are stuck in a lower dwelling, they may begin to abuse us verbally. Pull away from them and know God is using us to enlighten them about where they need to be.)

- Reflection of God's life from within (We now are becoming more illuminating to others which might cause us to be highly persecuted.)

- Awareness that very few understand us now

- Knowledge that Jesus is beginning to fill us with His intellectual Gifts

- Faith in living our Baptism commitment

- A need for spiritual direction

- A desire to better understand our Catholic Faith (We know we must help Jesus bring others up the mountain with solid truth.)

- A deeper desire to be in intimate prayer with Jesus

- Praying the Scriptures daily

- Praying the Scriptures with the Holy Spirit as He is explaining the Word to us (We might begin having a desire to pray the divine office with the entire church.)

- Love for the Catholic Faith (Our roots are very strong now.)

- Believing more in faith and moving less on feelings

- Deepened reason based on the intellectual Gifts of the Holy Spirit

- Discipline of ourselves to reflect the Fruits of God's life instead reflecting dysfunctional behavior

- Awareness that our love for God is growing rapidly (We are seeing His love for us. This intimate relationship is very sweet and honored by God.)

- Prayer life that is more meditative instead of vocal

- Pondering many books that fill the intellect with knowledge

- Learning how to detach from anything that takes you from Him

- Learning to see as God sees through the Spirit (Do not see life just through your natural eyes. Seeing this way leads us into viewing things literally instead of spiritually. The Holy Spirit speaks to us through symbolic words. The Bible is filled with symbolism, Take time to learn the meaning behind the symbolism.)

- Living life knowing this purgation will end and we will enter the glory of God Himself

Areas in us that need to be purged in the fifth dwelling:

- A desire to abandon prayer because we feel like God does not hear us (This is just a feeling, and the truth is that He is closer to us now in this fifth dwelling than He was in the past dwellings. Not only is He closer to us, but also we are closer to Him, so our intercessory prayer is sweeter to Him.

- A desire to ignore the wounded areas the Holy Spirit is bringing up within us

- Holding the person or persons who wounded us bound to the abuse (Ask God to help us heal the grudge that we might have.)

- Inability to deal with the illusions we have created, not even realizing that we live in illusions

- A desire to stop going to the Sacraments (This desire is strong in the fifth dwelling because we feel God has abandoned us. He has not abandoned us. He is showing us areas that we need to look at so that we can heal and enter deeper into Him.)

- A desire to make life-changing decisions such as quitting a job, getting a divorce, quitting the priesthood or leaving the convent (Our lives at this point are very dry. God allows this feeling so that we keep focused on the areas that are keeping us away from Him and blocking us from entering Him deeper. If we deal with the effects of our wounds and we are healed, God will once again reveal Himself to us.)

- An urge to fight against the purging process with alcohol or drugs (Vices prolong the purging process.)

When we enter the sixth dwelling, God brings us so close to Him that we begin to desire to die just to be with Him and Him alone. He allows us to feel this way so that we learn how never to offend Him again. He brings us into the first Commandment, to love God with all our heart, mind, soul, and strength.

Spiritual Notes

Lamb of God
Who Takes Away the Sins of the World

The Sixth Dwelling of Purgatory:

The sixth door opens: Jesus says, "Come Forward!"

The sixth dwelling begins our engagement in Christ Jesus. This dwelling is a joyful one; however, Joy is only experienced when we are with Christ. When in public, our trials are more severe. Many misunderstand us and are cruel to us for no reason. We experience much persecution from those who were once close to us. This dwelling teaches us about the life we are now living in Christ Jesus. We learn how the world has reflected evil and how we have walked the path, working very hard to remain pure for Jesus. The days are lived now with us looking at all the areas we do not want to go into because we worked so hard to remain innocent. We cling to God, and He allows us to cling to Him. God wants us as His own with no one but Him attached to us. He allows this so that we never leave Him again.

In our prayer life, we might experience Jesus explaining and revealing the Scriptures to us. He reveals the way the Holy Spirit speaks through the hidden symbols that veil others. He explains the parables so that we understand them clearly. He begins to reveal His life and the hidden meanings of Scripture that very few see.

We are now living a life very intimately united to Him. This life is very secret and loving on both sides. Our spirit is slowly entering into His Holy Spirit to become one Spirit.

What We Might Experience in the Middle of This Dwelling
We may experience many trials, but the trials do not seem to bother us much anymore. In fact, we welcome them, knowing that with every trial the light of God is being revealed through us. We take the trials and tribulations as a great compliment from God instead of a great burden as we once took them. The effects of Satan are almost gone now. We

have much self-control. We stay above and far in front of evil. We can see evil coming but know how to deal with it sooner now. God is using us to bring much light into the world. Our desire is to serve Him and to love Him completely now. Our desire is on fire to satisfy His needs in others so that they too can get to know, love, and serve Him. Some of us are so in love with Him that we experience a pain in our hearts and a longing to be in Him and with Him forever. This pain of desire that reflects love replaces the sting of death that once lived in us. Sin in our souls is minimal. Mortal sin is far gone. We live so as not to offend in any way, but being in the human body still wakens us, and we do fall into venial sin.

This venial sin to the souls in the sixth dwelling is so strong that we long to get absolution.

Our souls walk so parallel with God that the little offenses we might see in ourselves are quickly remedied. In the beginning dwellings, many souls justify offenses and think little of them.

Yet the souls in this sixth dwelling feel they are offending God even when He might not be offended. This belief is very good; it places souls in a humble, pure state, desiring never to offend God. We enter prayer often in the sixth dwelling. (When I say to enter prayer in the sixth dwelling, I mean to enter the inner room; there still is a door to enter in the sixth dwelling. The souls that dwell in the sixth dwelling of purgatory still need to enter prayer through a door to meet our Prince in the inner room. If these souls pass from this life to the next, they immediately go into the center room of Heaven to rest in Him forever.)

There is one area in this sixth dwelling that needs to be purified. It is the desire to leave Earth and be in Heaven with God. Many souls in the sixth dwelling neglect themselves in being healthy. They lose their desire to be on Earth. This feeling needs to be purged. Our desire for God is very strong, but what about our sisters and brothers? If we leave in this beautiful state, who will be able to illuminate the Fruits and Gifts and bring them to Earth? These souls do not realize the need to stay to do the work. This longing for God deep within our souls begins to increase so much that our only wish is to pass and be with God immediately. Nothing seems to satisfy the soul. The desire these souls have to be with God completely is also God's desire. This veil is very thin, and the longing for it to be removed has reached the point of wanting to die right now to be with God. As this dwelling ends, the Holy Spirit unites itself with the spirit of the soul. This uniting of the two is the beginning of the seventh dwelling.

Areas in us that need to increase in the sixth dwelling:

- Peaceful prayer life as we are beginning to hear the voice of God instruct us
- Instructions from God on how to accomplish His mission through us
- Knowing our Hearts will be pierced and wounded with the love of God himself (This wounding is what makes our longing for God at this point almost unbearable here on Earth.)
- Walking very cautiously so as not to offend our beloved Lord
- Love for the Church and all she teaches
- A desire to attend daily Mass
- A need for the Sacrament of Reconciliation
- Prayer life that is very sweet and filled with peace and rest
- Deep contemplation as Jesus profoundly engages us
- Daily thoughts about God and His ways
- Dreams that confirm our current lives in the Blessed Trinity
- Closeness to all the Saints and those who have passed on
- Illumination to others of God's Gifts and Fruits living within us and reflecting through us
- A desire to serve God in our neighbors and to fill the needs of our brothers and sisters so that they can also know, love, and serve God
- Knowledge that others need to be loved by God (We go to great lengths to serve others in the love that God has for us.)
- Knowledge that God is well pleased with us
- Acceptance that all areas that needed purging are now being purged (However, this purging is not as confusing and pain-filled; it is willful detachment.)
- Knowledge that the Holy Spirit is illuminating us with intellectual Gifts
- Knowledge that the veils are being lifted as we begin to see as God sees
- Knowledge that We now can enter the prayer of rest
- Knowledge that we are very near to our beloved Lord, resting in His peace and in His joy
- A desire and longing to die and to be with God completely

- Loving God above all and in all. (We must love Him more than our Divine Missions in Him.)
- Knowing His loving Hand and trusting Him through the pain of detaching

Areas in us that need to be purged in the sixth dwelling:

- Neglecting ourselves because our focus is so deep in Christ (As we grow in the life of Christ, we begin to see how important it is to be in good health to be better servants to our Lord.)
- A desire to be alone so as not to fall into sin (God needs us to serve Him in others. He does not need us to walk in fear in any way.)
- Knowing that a very thin veil is still covering the knowledge of God in us (We must still cooperate with the Holy Spirit in revealing the complete truth of God's life and what He expects us to do for Him in serving Him in others.)

Redemption Process That We Enter

There will be times when Jesus asks us to suffer with Him. This time of suffering is immense, but this immense suffering is used to help save other souls that might have entered into hell forever. The best way to describe this suffering in the life of Christ is that "Jesus is stripped, nailed, and crucified!" I call this stage "entering into the abyss to save others from entering hell." How much is one stripped, nailed, and crucified? Do we enter here and cooperate to be stripped, nailed, and crucified to share in the sufferings of redemption to help our Lord? Sharing in the redemption process in the life of Christ brings the soul to feeling as if it is completely empty and very weak. At this point in sharing the redemption process, the weakness one might experience is the strength of God in the soul. There will be times where we want to die. The misery of the vast abyss is so deep and empty that one cries out, "Lord, why have you forsaken me and left me to die in my misery? What have I done to deserve this much pain?" No answer comes! We are left in this vast abyss to suffer the agony of the cross, a cross that belongs to others who we are helping in their spiritual lives. One might cry out, "Was not my cross enough? Must I suffer this too, alone? Who can be saved? Must the curtain be torn from top to bottom? Who can be saved, and where are they? Who are they?" Many souls benefit from this redemption process. for it is when we are weak that God is strong in and through us.

Prayer:

O Lord, deliver me in You so that I may deliver you through me.

After we return to our works in the Lord, we understand that those for whom we have been praying are graced with increased enlightenment.

You Have Died and Your Life is Hidden with Christ in God…
Col. 3: 1-4

Brothers and sisters: If then you were raised with Christ, seek what is above, where Christ is seated at the right hand of God. Think of what is above, not of what is on earth. For you have died and your life is hidden with Christ in God. When Christ your life appears, then you too will appear with Him in Glory.

Our Mission in Christ…

At the end of the sixth dwelling, He will appear to us with our mission. Once we see Him, we enter the seventh dwelling; the two spirits become one spirit in Christ. We are united, like two strings completely entwined as one string. We do not know where one begins and the other ends. Instead of wanting to die to be with Him forever, we now know we must bring the glory of God Himself down the mountain to fill the Earth as it is in Heaven and to help Jesus bring others up the mountain.

In the prodigal son story, the father and the son enter the house; the father puts a ring on his son and kills the fat calf to celebrate the homecoming. This homecoming in Abba and this constant remaining in Christ is the celebration of Eucharist as one Body in Christ.

He will put a spiritual ring on our finger because we have entered complete union in Him. As St. Paul said, "It is no longer I that live, but Christ Jesus through me." This union of two becoming one is complete, as complete as the relationship can be here on Earth. The sting of death in the souls who enter this seventh dwelling no longer exists. Death and its sting have no hold on these beautiful souls. All the work of being purged is done, and now the soul can enter Christ and commune with Him forever. We can witness these beautiful souls in their incorruptible state. There is no process of rot to the bodies. They are at rest in their Father's embrace forever. The work of purgation is complete. They now have free access into Paradise forever, resting in all the goodness of God and His creation.

At the end of the sixth dwelling, we will get a visit from heaven. I know three doctors of the Church who talk about this visit. Many saints have seen Christ at the end of the sixth dwelling. Some were pierced with the wounds of Christ; some were given a ring, but all were instructed about their Divine Mission to bring to Earth what is in Heaven, just as our Blessed Mother was instructed.

This visit tells us of our Divine Mission in Christ Jesus. His visit to us will confirm our union in Him. Some call this visit an engagement of the two spirits entering into one. Some call this visit a piercing of the heart because He wounds us in the deepest center of our being with His Love, uniting Him to us forever. Our Blessed Mother Mary and her Divine Mission was the first Divine Mission to bring us into our own Divine Missions in Christ.

We emulate her Divine Mission by entering into our center, the womb of our temple where the Blessed Trinity dwells to bring to light the epiphany of God's Life in us.

Our Divine Missions are full of revelations of the Life of Christ that is manifested through, with, and in us to reveal the Life of the Blessed Trinity within us. Whether it is through corporal or spiritual works, His full glory in us is revealed here on Earth as it is in Heaven. Look at the saints and see how they revealed the glory of God in their individual saintly lives. Realize that their works, whether spiritual or corporal, brought all into knowing God as God is—Love in Him and in one another.
Tell the Good News. Announce the way of the Lord to all that we meet so that all can know, love, and serve Him as well.

Spiritual Notes

Lamb of God
Who Takes Away the Sins of the World

The Seventh Dwelling, Heaven: Union with God

Jesus says, "Come Forward!"

Revelation 3:8-11
I know all the things you do, and I have opened a door for you that no one can shut. You have little strength, yet you obeyed my word and did not deny me. Look! I will force those who belong to Satan--those liars who say they are Jews but are not--to come and bow down at your feet. They will acknowledge that you are the ones I love.

All the doors are open to us in the lower dwellings…

The King of Kings: Rev. 19: 11
The Heavens were opened, and as I looked on, a white horse appeared; its rider was called "The Faithful and True."

Entering the seventh dwelling, the souls who are still walking the Earth in body are free in Christ; they have no door to the inner chamber or inner room. It is only in the seventh dwelling that the souls are so pure in Christ that they never leave the inner room. They can come and go freely whenever they like. They can go in and out of any dwelling to help their sisters and brothers in Christ and never be affected by the evil that might linger in that dwelling. The devil has no hold on them. Their works are done in communion with God. At this point, they never leave Him. They can enter deep into prayer whenever they want to rest and be refreshed in Him; He is always aware of their being in Him and is very attentive to them. Whenever He needs them, they are ready to serve Him by serving others. They lack nothing of what they might need to minister to a needy soul. All the Fruits and Gifts are free for them to minister. The Holy Spirit is at work and speaking through them to gather and feed His flock. These souls in the seventh dwelling are free to enter Heaven and receive all wisdom from Heaven and all the help they might need from those who are in Heaven. Their prayers are fruitful because they dwell in Christ and reflect Him with nothing repugnant to darken the reflection. They are clothed with His victory and speak with His Wisdom that many in this world desire to hear.

We will know when we are around these saints who are in the seventh dwelling; they naturally bring the Holy Spirit's pure illumination wherever they go. Very few words need to be spoken when we are around them.

We know what we need to do to become holier. They reflect all of Heaven and its glory here on Earth. These souls have everything at their disposal for them to minister.

The Fruits and Gifts of God are easy to see in these souls. They reflect them with great joy, uniting the Gifts so perfectly to be given out to serve the one they love, God. They serve Him by serving Him in others. Now the desire is not to die to be with God, but to help the Lord to get everyone else into this dwelling.

When we enter the seventh dwelling, we have two things at hand. One is an apron to put on to serve and the other is constant communion. We never leave Him now. Our works are done as Mary being in Martha and Martha being in Mary. Martha never goes any-where without Mary. Mary is the perfect intimacy with Jesus, and Martha is the perfect Host of Christ to minister to Christ in others.

Prayer is very deep; the body is now suspended in the life of God through prayer. This deep contemplative prayer becomes a resting in Glory. The Glory is Abba! He is filling us with His Divine Life. We melt in Him as He embraces us and brings us to Him. It is very important we enter this deep prayer daily to stay restored in Him. God created the world for man and woman to be united to Him in Spirit and to rest in His Glory of Goodness forever. We rest with Him and appreciate all that He created, for all that God created is good. He rests in that goodness and wants us to rest with Him. This resting is a complete immersion into Christ Jesus who is peace, the peace that Christ came to deliver to us. This resting is entering into the inheritance of our Baptism. Contemplation is our communing with God and centering prayer in God continuously, night and day, contemplating Him and His way.

It is the seventh dwelling, or the seventh day, that is as Holy as God is Holy; it is the day of rest. But this day is not a day as we know it. It is forever the day of rest for us, never leaving communion in Him. Eucharist, which is Jesus Christ, is the center of Heaven; Jesus Christ is the tree of Life. The Sacraments continually give us the Fruit of His life, which is Grace, so that we can enter His life and rest with Abba. The seventh dwelling is our union with the unblemished Lamb, the one who takes away the sin of the world and delivers us into the arms of Abba. The actions of the Holy Spirit purge us with the fire of Love. This love, which is Jesus, was brought down from Heaven to deliver us into complete love, which is Abba. We are in Union; the bride unites her spirit with His Spirit and they become one in Christ, united by the Holy Spirit to rest in Abba forever. In this seventh dwelling, we do not need a door to enter as we do in the other dwellings. We are free to enter into, rest, and be with Him always.

The New Jerusalem
Revelation 21: 1-3   9-14
Then I saw a new heaven and a new Earth, for the old heaven and the old Earth had disappeared. And the sea was also gone. And I saw the holy city, the New Jerusalem, coming down from God out of heaven like a beautiful bride prepared for her husband. I heard a loud shout from the throne, saying, "Look, the home of God is now among his people! He will live with them, and they will be his people. Then one of the seven angels who held the seven bowls containing the seven last plagues came and said to me, "Come with me! I will show you the bride, the wife of the Lamb." So he took me in spirit to a great, high mountain, and he showed me the holy city, Jerusalem, descending out of heaven from God.
It was filled with the glory of God and sparkled like a precious gem, crystal clear like jasper.
Its walls were broad and high, with twelve gates guarded by twelve angels. And the names of the twelve tribes of Israel were written on the gates. There were three gates on each side--east, north, south, and west. The wall of the city had twelve foundation stones, and on them was written the names of the twelve apostles of the Lamb.

Every time we enter into Mass, all seven cups or seven chalices are on the Altar. All seven dwellings and those who are in them are free to enter into heaven through the Blood of the unblemished Lamb. He takes away the sin of the world and allows them to enter heaven. Most of them do not understand what is taking place at Mass. Jesus is transforming us into Himself and taking us into Heaven. All seven dwellings are taken up and delivered. All seven bowls are filled with the Spirit of wine that is transformed into the blood of the unblemished Lamb.

Jesus takes us with Him to be delivered into heaven. We must enter Mass in full union with the Holy Spirit, with our eyes closed and our hearts lifted. The eyes of our souls must be fixed on Jesus. We do not go to Mass; we enter into Mass. We enter into the Lamb of God who takes away the sins of the world and delivers us through Himself into

Abba's arms. Heaven is now! The seventh dwelling is living in this transformation of Union at all times. We commune with God as God communes with us.

Worship in Heaven
Revelation 4:1-6
After this, I looked and saw an open door to Heaven, and I heard the trumpet-like voice which had spoken to me before. It said, "Come up here and I will show we what must take place in time to come." At once I was caught up in ecstasy. A throne was standing there in heaven, and on the throne was seated One whose appearance had a gemlike sparkle as of jasper and carnelian. Around the throne was a rainbow as brilliant as emerald. Surrounding the throne were twenty-four other thrones in a circle around that throne. And on each of these thrones there was an elder dressed in white clothes and wearing a gold crown. From the thrown came flashes of lightning and roars of thunder; before it burned seven flaming torches, the seven spirits of God. The floor around the throne was like a sea of glass that was crystal clear.

When we enter Mass in and through the Holy Spirit, we are caught in the ecstasy of Jesus. The brilliant emerald is symbolic of Heaven and Earth filled with His beautiful colors of Glory. Now we can see with crystal clearness the secrets of Heaven. All is revealed, and now we see a new Heaven and a new Earth.

The New Heaven and the New Earth
Revelation 21: 1-5
Then I saw a new heaven and a new Earth. The former heaven and the former Earth had passed away, and the sea was no more. I also saw the holy city, a new Jerusalem, coming down out of heaven from God, prepared as a bride adorned for her husband. I heard a loud voice from the throne saying, "Behold, God's dwelling is with the human race. He will dwell with them and they will be his people and God himself will always be with them (as their God). He will wipe every tear from their eyes, and there shall be no more death or mourning, wailing or pain, (for) the old order has passed away." The one who sat on the throne said, "Behold, I make all things new."

As we enter into Heaven at Mass, we are transformed deeper and deeper into the unblemished Lamb. Because we have entered pure, our soul being as white as when we entered Baptism, He enters into us as one Body and one Spirit in Christ forever. This beautiful communion never ends. We are completely free to be in Him forever.

In the Upper Room: The Turn Around
Luke 22: 31-32
"Simon, Simon, behold Satan has demanded to sift all of you like wheat, but I have prayed that your own faith may not fail; and once you have turned back, you must strengthen our brothers."

When we enter the seventh mansion, we learn how to love and serve our neighbor. We go down the mountain to serve our Lord in the least of our brothers and sisters to strengthen them so they too can make the journey up the mountain through these purgation dwellings.

Revelation 22: 1-5
The angel showed me a river that was crystal clear, and its waters gave life. The river came from the throne where God and the Lamb were seated. Then it flowed down the middle of the city's main street. On each side of the river are trees that grow a different kind of fruit each month of the year. The fruit gives life, and the leaves are used as medicine to heal the nations. God's curse will no longer be on the people of that city. He and the Lamb will be seated there on their thrones, and its people will worship God and will see him face to face. God's name will be written on the foreheads of the people. Never again will night appear, and no one who lives there will ever need a lamp or the sun. The Lord God will be their light, and they will rule forever.

In this seventh dwelling, God is telling us that all the Gifts and the Fruits of His Divine Life are medicine to heal the nations. These nations are the other dwellings. All those who are living in them are being purged from the curse of the sin where they dwell. God will use us in this dwelling to enter back into all the previous dwellings. We can enter, and the evil that dwells there in these shallower dwellings has no effect on us. The curse that the other souls are in is not affecting us. We have the life-giving fruit trees of God's full life living in the middle of our union with God. God's curse will no longer affect us. What we need for the souls who dwell in the shallower dwellings is to help them be purged, like rivers constantly flowing to help us heal others. These rivers are the seven Sacraments, constantly flowing with Grace to heal and restore the souls to their Baptismal state in the image and likeness of God.

Blessed are they who enter here. Blessed are those who are pure of heart, for they shall see God face to face. In this seventh dwelling, many Mystical Gifts are given to us. Many! Remain in God as God is in us forever and ever. Amen.

The Upper Room and the Lesson of True Humbleness in Service to God Who Is in All . . .

When the Apostles were in the upper room with Jesus, He took an apron and tied it around Himself. Then He took a basin and a pitcher and began to wash the feet of the Apostles. When we enter this seventh dwelling, we make the turn around. We must put on a spiritual apron and tie it around us and then take a spiritual basin and a pitcher and begin to wash the feet of all those who are climbing the mountain. This washing of the feet prepares them to make the journey up the mountain. All the doors in the shallower dwellings are open to us. We know what others are going through even if they lock us out of their lives. We can see why they are locking us out.

We now know as God knows, and we see as God sees, what Heavenly food they need to grow in the good health of Jesus. We fill the needs in all those we meet so that they, too, can climb the mountain and enter His rest. When we walk to serve Jesus in the least of our brothers and sisters, we always walk in humble service.

I Want Us to See with Eyes of Faith

Enter into Him, as He is already in us. As we lose ourselves and all we created that has tricked us into falsehood, we must enter into our Baptismal promise to reject all of evil and the glamour of it. As we lose ourselves, we sell all that keeps us focused on ourselves instead of on Him so that we can find who we really are. We are an image, a likeness of God, and nothing more. He is God; He created the heavens and the Earth. We create nothing, for everything has already been created by God, and it is done perfectly in Him who is all perfection.

It is so wonderful to be nothing and to rest in God. We rest in Him and share who He is. Everything, all in all, is so very good.

He allows us to share in His Life of Glory that is all good. We do not deserve it; we do not earn it; we fell from Grace; we left our home in Him and all of His Truth. We now have returned, and we now know our Abba and the home we have in Him. Praise Him, Thank Him, but most of all, Love Him.

Revelation 22:17
The Spirit and the bride say, "Come!" Everyone who hears this should say, "Come!" If you are thirsty, come! If you want life-giving water, come and take it. It's free! Come and enter heaven now. It's free!

Entering Union in the seventh dwelling:

We have entered into God as God is in us. His Fruitful life is now in full bloom. We enter into our Divine Mission of the predestined sanctified life that God prepared us for. We are now on the top of the mountain resting in God as God rests in us.

We are in the "turn around" where we help all the others who are in the shallower dwellings. No doors are locked for us to help anyone. We can now see in others what God sees in them to help them through their dwelling.

We are free; we do not have any stumbling blocks.

We do not experience any more purging pains, persecutions, and redemption sufferings.

Evil has no hold on us. We can enter any dwelling with no effects of evil.

Prayer life is simple and beautiful and very deep. We experience, deep joy, deep peace, and tremendous tranquility.

We experience the Blessed Trinity as three natures, yet one God in the entire universe. The heavens are in perfect harmony, rotating or spirating from the center of God's Life. This center brings us into the Body of God and its entire array. The array that we rest in is the glory of God and the love that He created in the heavens and the Earth. All is in God, and God is in all. This resting brings us the deep love of God and neighbor, for all are one.

Our bodies are suspended in prayer and we enter into God's glory to be filled with His glory.

We enter ecstasy, but we do not react to it as we did in the sixth dwelling. Prayer leaves us in complete peace.

The Fruit of prayer now fills us with complete joy.

We can enter deep into prayer easily at anytime, for now our entire lives are a prayer. We can go up the mountain to be in God as God is in us any time we desire Him.

We can see what stumbling blocks others are facing in the other six dwellings, and we can help them through this sight. (This sight is called "seeing as God sees.")

We can hear God fully communing with us, night and day.

All things that we might need to help others in their dwellings are at our disposal.

We enter into knowing the Holy Trinity and how the three divine persons work as one. They are very distinct, but They are One.

Others' thoughts are laid open to us. We know before they speak what their souls are saying.
Angels are constantly bringing us others to hold in prayer.

We have knowledge of those who have passed on that are helping us.

We are on fire with the desire for our sisters and brothers to enter the seventh dwelling. We can help our sisters and brothers by serving our King of Kings.

Our longing for God is now the longing for everyone to enter Heaven.

We no longer are corrected in Scripture as in the shallower dwellings; we are confirmed in our words by God's Word. The words we speak are resurrected within three days for others to have confirmation by the Holy Spirit Himself.

Others who are around us receive confirmations from what we have told them to do concerning their growth in Jesus.

We reflect many Fruits and Gifts of God's life living in us. We do not need to say too much; the light of God says it for us.

Our bodies in prayer start to break down.

Prayer becomes deeper and more intense; His breath is the Holy Spirit overshadowing us.

We may experience spirating in union with the universe, for all is one now. This spiration of our being is our whole being resting in the spiration of the love of God and all that He created. As the Holy Spirit spirates, or moves in love, so do we because of the complete union.

Dreams are no longer dreams as we once knew them to be. Now, dreams are a communing with God all night. We contemplate Him night and day, day and night, and never leave Him. We are in Eucharist all the time, entering into Him and experiencing His full peace and complete joy in communion with us.

We get Heavenly messages to explain what God wants of us today. These messages are divine and help many.

God constantly reassures us of His presence within us in times of turmoil.

The Holy Spirit is the one who speaks through us so we do not have to worry about what to say.

Our trials and tribulations bring much redemption for others.

Our periods of sharing in Jesus' redemption produce much Fruit for all of our prayers. This redemption pain that we share through Christ brings us into the Garden of Gethsemane. We know that the pain is not our purification; instead, we are suffering through, with, and in Christ for the world.

Our specific predestined mission is now in full bloom, branching out for all to benefit. It is like the small mustard seed that grows into a huge tree where all the birds rest in its branches.

We enjoy the ability to be free in God as God is free in us.

Our Rest in God (as God is resting in us) is very deep, intimate, and refreshing.

We are so absorbed in God and all of His beauty that we get lost in His Love. This is what takes place in the suspension of the body. We lose all sense of the body and enter into the Spirit and get lost in God as God is.

Scripture is translated to us with all the symbolic meaning fully understood.

We hear as God hears. We hear God, and we can hear what a soul might need without asking.

We see as God sees. We see God in all things and in everyone.

We know as God knows. We know all things and what might keep another from entering deeper into the life of Christ. Others stumbling blocks are clear to us so that we can help others rid themselves of their stumbling blocks.

We lack nothing and desire nothing but to serve, love, and know God.

We dread offending God, so we try to remain pure, humble, holy, and as innocent as God Himself.

We are very close to God in His Word, Christ Jesus in the Sacraments, and the teachings of the Church. We see how He confirms us through Scripture.

God's Word is coming alive in us for us to minister to others and to bring them deeper into Him.

We bring others to know, love, and serve our Lord.

Our hearts are always on fire with love for Jesus, melting in Him as one whenever possible.

We acknowledge that love is the greatest virtue. Our desire in the seventh dwelling is centered more on helping others than experiencing the Glory for ourselves. Our desire is to stay in the body to serve others. In the prayer of rest, we are elevated into Heaven, and it is in God that we rest. We get to be refreshed in Abba's love. This love fills us to serve the Lord in our brothers and sisters.

Matthew 8: 1-3
When Jesus came down from the mountain, great crowds followed him. And then a leper approached, did him homage, and said, "Lord, if you wish, you can make me clean." He stretched out his hand, touched him, and said, "I will do it. Be made clean." His leprosy was cleansed immediately.

As We Make the Turn and Come Down the Mountain to Serve our Lord in Others
We are not only getting to know God as God is, but we are also getting to know where God has these souls and what they are doing to remain veiled. When we make the turn to go down the mountain to encourage and strengthen those who are in the lower dwellings, we are serving God by helping the Holy Spirit by His enlightenment. This enlightenment brings light to the blind who are veiled in darkness from the sin and pain that keep them bound to the dark instead of allowing them to enter into God's glory. Those who enter the

seventh dwelling can now see as God sees. Their Divine Mission enables them to work in and with the Holy Spirit in the purgation process. Jesus told the Apostles in the upper room that they were not here to be served, but to serve.

We as His servants must help one another in the redemption process to bring them up the mountain of transfiguration. Remember, we must remain solid on the rock that is Christ the Church, always being faithful to the Sacraments to be sustained in the life of Christ.

Any hardship that Satan uses to tempt us will be overcome by the Grace that will sustain us. "Take [these hardships] from me Lord," Paul prayed; and the Lord said, "My Grace is sufficient." God's Grace is what sustains us in the life of trials and tribulations. Satan has no hold on a soul that is filled with Grace.

Enter into Him, as He is already in us, losing ourselves and all we created that has tricked us into falsehood. We must enter into our Baptismal promise to reject all evil and the glamour of it. We must lose ourselves in God and sell all that keeps us attached to the flesh. As we enter Him and worship Him through the Spirit who is truth, we can find who we really are, a reflection of Jesus. We can then rest in Him and be allowed to share who He is—**EVERYTHING**.

We do not have to wait to die physically to enter Heaven; Jesus came to Earth to open the Heavens for us. All we need to do is cooperate with Him through the workings of His Holy Spirit that lives in us.

Our Prayer Life . . .
It is here in this seventh dwelling that the knowing we once experienced in the sixth dwelling becomes the actual voice of God. He now instructs us face-to-face and shares with us all the goodness of creation. Our prayer life begins with His breath filling us, surrounding us in a cloud. It is in this cloud that we begin to see as God sees and to know as God knows all the secrets of heaven. The sword has been lifted, and we are allowed to enter into the goodness of Abba, Home for all eternity. The fire that once purged us is now the glory of God Himself. Our prayer life is that of resting in all of His goodness, being refreshed with His glorious life that now penetrates every inch of us.

We lose the sense of our body because we are now elevated in His Divine Spirit. We are taken up into the highest heavens. The joy we experience is complete, and the peace we encounter is radiating all around us, illuminating our being in God as God is all Radiant Glory. As we go down the mountain to serve the needs of our brothers and sisters, all dwellings are now opened to us with no door to block us from entering. We see as God sees, and we know as God knows. Our whole being is now in union with the entire universe. We move in complete harmony with the creation of God. His glory is penetrating us with Divine Life.

Before ending the dwellings, I want to bring us into what I have experienced in the deepest dwelling where God has brought me. When I enter His rest in me, I come into the Spirit and truth of who I am—a nothing. My physical eyes are shut to the material world; I am not a part of that world. I have left to follow Him. I have lost myself completely to find myself in God. Please hear me. I hear His breath; it consumes me and surrounds me, bringing me deeper into His rest. His breath is my breath. When I rest in Him, He allows me to share in all of His glory and He radiates His Love in me and through me to fill me with His Divine Grace. I get lost in the beauty of the radiation; it consumes me. His Body is the universe. He does not rotate; the universe rotates. We rotate in harmony. All around Him, the rotation is the Love of Spiration that we experience as we enter the life of the Holy Spirit. When we enter into Him who is Love, we feel the motion of Life rotating in the Mass of Glory.

God's Glory itself is what gives life to all things. I am no longer a separate body. I am in this Mass of Glory that is in all of us, and we are all in God. We no longer are separate bodies; we are one body in God. This Mass of Glory fills me with the Truth of all in all; this is the illuminating light of His Being. All that we see is His Truth, and all of His Truth fills us with the Truth of who He is. The joy and the peace are so intoxicating. I lose my body and its existence. I desire nothing, and I am very happy to exist in Him and all of His goodness with nothing of mine to interfere. He allows me to enter deep into His Life. It is hard to come back into my physical body. In this radiant rest, there is no more pain, for the work here in this seventh day, or the seventh dwelling, is completed. In the seventh day, I rest in all of His goodness. His peace embraces me, and His goodness fills me with tremendous joy. When I am resting in God, I am completely free to enter into Him to rest and be refreshed at anytime.

All that is of God and His Divine Image and Likeness that we now reflect here on Earth as it is in Heaven is within us. In the seventh dwelling, we enter the upper room, or the top of the mountain where we learn the second Commandment, to love our neighbor as ourselves. We put on the apron of service, and we take with us a cloth to wash and prepare the feet of all those whom we will meet as we go down the mountain to serve the Lord in the least of our brothers and sisters in Christ. We are now preparing them to be elevated in the Life of Jesus by washing their feet to climb the mountain and be transformed deeper and deeper into His image and likeness, so that they too can come to know, love, and serve our Lord.

My previous book, *Straight Street to Heaven*, teaches us what we need to do to get through the dwellings as easily as we can.

This book, *Spiration of Love,* teaches us what we will experience when we go through each dwelling. Each one of us must go through the dwellings without getting trapped so as to slow the process of the purgation that allows us to enter into the Pure Lamb of God, Jesus Christ. I hope and I pray that all who apply these truths to their lives will encounter true union with Jesus for all eternity.

God Bless all of you,
Victoria Rose Pisano

All that I am. . .

Nothing from nothing

equals nothing

For that's all that I am

But even this nothing

In Abba

Becomes everything

Through

Jesus Christ our Lord

Amen ...

Victoria Rose Pisano

Spiritual Notes

Spiritual Notes

To continue on your personal journey to a closer union with God, please take a moment to review the following classes and personal instruction provided by the author, Victoria Rose Pisano:

Straight Street to Heaven

Victoria walks her students through a seven week course discussing in detail the dwellings of purgatory as discussed in Spiration of Love, as well as what one needs to do to fully cooperate with the Holy Spirit to achieve union with God. The seven two-hour sessions are supplemented by Victoria's workbook, Straight Street to Heaven. Her classroom setting is intimate and affords ample time for instruction as well as the opportunity to question Victoria on areas of uncertainty. As moving through each dwelling is a process, so is the process of learning. Therefore, many of Victoria's students return for further instruction and guidance.

Dream Analysis

The Holy Spirit speaks to us through symbolism that is sometimes not easy to understand. Victoria, through her gift of prophecy, can help students interpret what the Holy Spirit is communicating to them through dreams in three main ways. She guides students in a direction bringing them closer to God, corrects areas keeping them blind and connected to dysfunction and sin or confirms and strengthens that they are on the right path. These three avenues not only lead to a higher level of understanding of the symbolism, but also help to unlock many repressed areas that can otherwise result in feelings of anxiety, depression confusion and isolation.

Order Form

Telephone orders: 440-886-5774

Email orders: straightstreet1@cox.net

Web Site orders: www.straightstreettoheaven.com
or www.halopublishing.com

Postal Orders:
Victoria Rose Pisano, 4405 Wood Thrush, Parma, OH 44134

- -

I want to order _____copies at $19.95 of *Spiration of Love* by Victoria Rose Pisano

Name: _____

Address: _____

City:_____ State:_____Zip: _____

Telephone:_____

Email Address: _____

Sales tax: Please add your city sales tax.

Shipping: U.S. $4.50 for the first book and $2.00 for each additional book.

International: $9.50 for the first book and $5.00 for each additional book.

Halo ● ● ● ●
Publishing International
www.halopublishing.com

Printed in the United States
150548LV00004B/1/P

9 781935 268031